1220

1

DATE DUE	

Productivity and
Quality
Improvement

Productivity and Quality Improvement

A Practical Guide to Implementing Statistical Process Control

John L. Hradesky
President, National Summit Group

McGraw-Hill Book Company

New York   St. Louis   San Francisco   Auckland   Bogotá
Caracas   Colorado Springs   Hamburg   Lisbon
London   Madrid   Mexico   Milan   Montreal
New Delhi   Oklahoma City   Panama   Paris
San Juan   São Paulo   Singapore
Sydney   Tokyo   Toronto

Library of Congress Cataloging-in-Publication Data

Hradesky, John L.
  Productivity and quality improvement.

  Includes index.
  1. Process control—Statistical methods.
I. Title.
TS156.8.H73   1987   658.5   87-16251
ISBN 0-07-030499-8

  34567890   DOC/DOC   9210

*The editors for this book were Betty Sun and Stephen M. Smith, the
designer was Naomi Auerbach, and the production supervisor was
Richard A. Ausburn. This book was set in Century Schoolbook. It
was composed by the McGraw-Hill Book Company Professional and
Reference Division composition unit.*

Printed and bound by R. R. Donnelley & Sons Company.

Contents

Preface

Due to foreign competition the United States is facing the challenge of improving its productivity and quality. Companies talk about such improvements, but few ever achieve them. Many say they have statistical process control (SPC), but what they really have is "quality veneer," and most are not satisfied with their implementation or results. This book is for these companies and any other company that wants to be successful with SPC.

To be successful a company must want to survive, and it must believe that if it takes no action to improve its products it will most likely fail. To survive a company must have a plan, ability to focus on the plan, and effective execution follow-up to ensure that the plan is working. The systematic productivity and quality improvement process was developed to meet this need.

Several books emphasize SPC, acceptance sampling, or design experiments. Others provide management concepts. This book is a composite of elements from many concepts and writings and emphasizes successful implementation of SPC with meaningful results. The concepts and techniques presented here allow a company to implement many facets of the Deming philosophy, a proven approach from which many companies have profited.

I dedicate this book to my wife Trish for her tolerance of my time-consuming obsession with the subject. Acknowledgments go to my father, Louis A. Hradesky, P.E., the late Albert Holzman, Ph.D., and W. Edwards Deming, Ph.D., for their influence through the years. I also acknowledge Michael deNicola, Robert Kleist, Elliott Glick, Ben Holt, and especially Jack Schwarzenbach from Printronix management for their roles in initially implementing the systematic productivity and quality improvement process, and Jack Dawson, Michael Millow, Ignacio Munoz, Wendell Paulson, Steve Wernick, and Tom Zimmerman for their participation in preparing the chapters. I also thank Tom Zimmerman for rewriting the chapters.

Introduction—The 12-Step Productivity and Quality Improvement Process

Over the years American industry has lost to overseas competition its position as the world's industrial leader. It must now regain lost markets or be transformed from an industrial giant to a giant importer. Industry must focus on what can be done now to reestablish an industrial base with unlimited potential. One proven technique developed in the United States, that can be used is *statistical process control (SPC)*. Japan has successfully applied it to management, quality, and productivity problems, but the success of SPC in the United States has been fleeting because executives and managers are not strongly committed to the technique and are not really *managing* the operations.

Productivity and Quality Improvement: A Practical Guide to Implementing Statistical Process Control takes the position that the lack of progress in improving quality, productivity, profits, and competitive edge is directly related to the lack of an integrated action plan for implementation of SPC. In other words, most executives do not know what to do, how to do it, or who should do it.

Effective SPC is 10% statistics and 90% management action and contains five key ingredients: (1) statistical techniques, (2) problem-solving techniques, (3) productivity and quality improvement leadership and attitudes, (4) quality planning, and (5) a systematic approach, which acts as the catalyst.

The main focus of this book is to provide a systematic approach to SPC implementation, which also ties together the other three ingredients. This approach is divided into 12 distinct yet related steps called *the 12-step productivity and quality improvement (PQI) process*. It is carried out by teams composed of department managers, supervisors, engineers, and key hourly personnel directly or indirectly associated with the product or processes being addressed. The teams are directed and supported by a steering committee of middle managers, who in turn report to an executive board of upper-level managers. The team concept conveys the message that PQI is everybody's business. The success or failure of the program is shared by all. Organizing for success then becomes an integral part of the program and a prerequisite for implementing SPC.

Here is a summary of the 12 steps.

Step 1. *Project identification.* This step defines the problem area clearly and develops a cost justification for the project, including a statement of the current or future impact of the problem and the opportunity for potential improvement. To further define the project, prepare a process flow diagram to help identify critical points in the process and the possible application of process control charts in other processes. Once the problem has been defined, as perceived by the internal customer or the end customer, the level of improvement is forecasted as a basis to justify the project. After the projected level of improvement has been quantified and approved, it becomes the target objective on performance measurement charts, which are created in step 3.

Step 2. *Planning and reporting.* This administrative step helps the project leader to manage the overall project. It is designed to keep the project on schedule in terms of timing and performing the project's goal. Three documents are created in this step: (a) A milestone plan, which lists each of the 12 steps, the project's scheduled start, and its completion date. (b) A progress report, which is updated weekly and evaluates the progress of the team in several key dimensions. A progress report is either a team report or a steering committee report. Both are issued within 24 hours after each meeting. (c) An annual PQI plan that identifies future projects and estimates of improvements in productivity and quality. The estimates are converted into dollars, and the plan is reviewed by management at an equal level of importance as the company sales plan and product plan. Another element of this step includes quarterly project presentations by the team leaders to the executive board for communication and motivational purposes.

Step 3. *Performance measurements.* This step establishes a method to measure performance in quality, productivity, or schedule relative to the customer's target objective. The major elements of the step are development of a measuring method, data collection, performance reporting, and charting progress.

Step 4. *Problem analysis and solution.* This step is the first directed at actual improvement of the process. We carry it out by applying recommended techniques such as events logs, diagnostic process audits, cause-and-effect diagrams, cause analysis, and design of experiments. These techniques will define causes and preventive actions for the problem(s) identified in step 1.

Step 5. *Inspection capability.* This step, called the missing link in SPC, is a technique for evaluating and quantifying the errors in inspection systems for variable or attribute data. It defines the criteria for accepting and rejecting any given inspection and test process, and sets the stage for the next step of the PQI process.

Step 6. *Process capability.* This step is a systematic procedure for determining the natural or inherent variation in a process. To measure and evaluate the true capability of a process, we apply statistical control chart methods. As in step 5, this step provides the team with criteria for accepting or rejecting a process and gives guidelines for corrective action. The power of this step is that it demonstrates whether the process is actually *capable* of meeting the targets established in step 1.

Step 7. *Corrective and preventive action matrix.* This step "closes the loop" in the application of SPC. It provides specific actions to bring the process back in control after it has gone out of control. The matrix lists all known defects and conditions that can exist in the process being measured along with their respective corrective and preventive (CP) actions. Its placement next to the process control chart eliminates guesswork and delay in initiating the CP action function.

Step 8. *Process control procedure.* This step documents the method for introducing and sustaining SPC. It establishes departmental responsibilities for the different activities associated with SPC, including installing, maintaining, and monitoring control charts, events logs, and CP action matrices. It also designates who is to do what when a process goes out of control.

Step 9. *Process control implementation.* Up to this point in the process only certain members of the operation have been involved in the project development. The intention of this step is to communicate and coordinate implementation of SPC with everyone identified in the process control procedure. The team holds a meeting to review a checklist of requirements, to confirm that all documentation has been completed, to make clarifications, and to secure commitment of responsibilities.

Step 10. *Problem prevention.* At this step the team tries to anticipate future problems and to develop the necessary preventive actions or contingency plans to deal with those problems. This step ensures that all gains will be maintained, and it provides valuable information for future improvement or breakthroughs to new performance levels. The failure mode effect analysis is used.

Step 11. *Defect accountability.* This step identifies and reports defect types and their sources. Defect sources are generally the same from industry to industry and can be categorized as workmanship, process, design, and component. Hand in hand with identification of problems, the recognition by the team and management of top performers must occur to ensure continued success.

Step 12. *Measurement of effectiveness.* Although each step of the process is verified before closure, measurement of effectiveness of the overall project is required to ensure that the desired results were achieved and that a plan exists to sustain the results. The team accomplishes measurement of effectiveness by conducting one or all of the following audits: process, product, systems, or financial.

The Appendix describes *quality targets,* through which customer requirements for the outgoing quality of the final product are achieved. This technique establishes individual workstation targets for quality levels and uses the final output quality target as the basis. It is the final team activity to ensure that the end-product quality meets customer requirements.

Preparing for Implementation

The expense of establishing new or different skills can be viewed as an insurmountable barrier if the current corporate culture works against the change. However, with proper preparation and execution of the guidelines and techniques in this book, a company can turn its investment into the best it has ever made.

The key to proper preparation of the plan is to educate all participants on SPC techniques, including the systematic 12-step PQI process. Although these statistical courses guarantee an effective start-up, they are merely prerequisite education. Other recommended reference materials are listed at the end of this book.

After the educational requirements have been fulfilled and the supporting structure has been installed, a critical process or product must be selected on which to implement SPC. The process or product should be challenging, allow successful implementation of SPC, and solve quality or productivity problems that are costing the company profits or customers. Selecting a team and strong team leader is very important for the success of SPC on the selected project.

If SPC is used as a management process rather than just another tool, significant results can be achieved. However, many pitfalls and obstacles are associated with successfully implementing SPC. The purpose of this book is to help users avoid those pitfalls, overcome the obstacles, and achieve success—that is, survive in business and make a profit.

Organizing for Successful Implementation

Successful implementation of the systematic 12-step PQI process is the result of change in the corporate culture. Only then will the desired improvements in productivity and quality be realized. Although the system described in this book has been successful in creating that change, there is no simple way of installing a system that will perpetuate itself. There is no pill to take that will fix what is there now. A company must be organized to learn to use SPC, execute the process, and solve its problems systematically. This section shows how to set up a successful PQI process implementation and development, including its organizational structure (roles and responsibilities within the structure), implementing with teams, and the roles of the facilitator and the advisor.

A typical organizational structure for the PQI process is illustrated in Fig. 1. This structure indicates that, especially in a large organization, more than one steering committee and several project teams may be functioning at the same time.

Organizational Structure

The first action a company must take to achieve the necessary change is to establish the organizational structure that will provide the foundation, direction, and support for PQI process implementation. Change begins at the top, and it will naturally cascade down to every level of the corporate structure. The organizational structure described in this section does not replace a company's existing structure but complements it. The main elements are the executive board, the steering committee, and the project team leaders and members.

Executive board

The executive board is the highest authority within the structure. Its principal members are the president and all vice presidents whose oper-

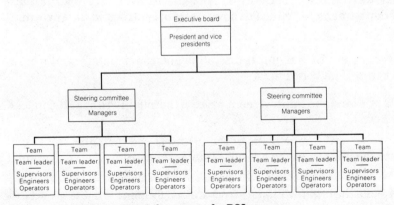

Figure 1 Typical organizational structure for PQI process.

ations directly influence the costs of quality relating to prevention of defects or errors, appraisal of conformance to specifications and requirements, internal failures, and external failures. The members usually come from product development, design engineering, manufacturing, quality control, customer service, and sometimes marketing and sales. The vice president of finance must also be included, to monitor and protect the company's investment in the program. The chairperson of the board (usually the president, executive vice president, or vice president of operations) controls the majority of the board's resources and thus has the most to gain from a successful program.

Because executive management (i.e., the executive board) plays a major role in the development and implementation of new systems that affect the way a company does business, we give some suggestions to help the board carry out its duties. In *Quality Without Tears*, Phil Crosby suggests that management must first establish the requirements it expects its employees to meet, and then must "supply the wherewithal that the employees need in order to meet these requirements." In point 9 of his famous "14 points," Dr. W. Edwards Deming says, "Break down the barriers between departments. People in research, design, sales and production must work as a team to foresee production and usage problems." Dr. J. M. Juran writes in *Upper Management and Quality* that "the job of upper management is to a large extent one of leading the company through three major breaks in tradition." Dr. Juran defines these breaks as follows:

1. *Annual improvement.*   Calls for a plan to improve quality each year.
2. *Hands-on leadership by upper management.*   Calls for the establishment of new policies, goals, plans, organization, measures, and controls.
3. *Massive training.*   The entire management team, not just the quality department, is trained in how to attain control and improve quality.

To implement SPC requires discipline and conviction from the executive board. The board must

1. Understand the improvement process thoroughly so that it can lead the way
2. Develop long-range plans of the future of the company and translate them into a living mission statement, a strategy, and an annual PQI plan
3. Provide the organizational structure and systems to achieve successful results

4. Select and develop personnel who will embrace the process and take a leadership role to achieve the goals

5. Assign responsibility and accountability to everyone involved and make sure that each person understands and is committed to his or her responsibility

6. Review and approve all projects to ensure either their compliance to the PQI implementation plan or the reasonableness of recovery plans to return the projects to schedule, and to maintain the focus of attention on critical and important objectives

7. Communicate values and high expectations clearly to everyone involved

8. Provide feedback on action plans, progress, and recovery plans, and support the teams through genuine interest, participation, reinforcement, and resources

9. Provide recognition and awards to encourage and sustain the improvement process (the process then becomes a way of life and replaces the old work activities)

10. Be sensitive to and aware of how its expectations might impact on others' needs about security, belonging, recognition, and quality of work life

11. Serve as a role model for the desired behavior by actively participating and supporting the objectives with more than words

The success of the organization depends on how well the board performs these functions, and how involved it is in the PQI process. Figure 2 pictures four possible perspectives the board can take.

Arm's length. The executive board wishes to have the program but finds itself delegating all authority and responsibility to lower levels.

Typical outcome. The process may initially be successful because of the efforts of middle management and the teams, but being starved for attention from upper management, will eventually die.

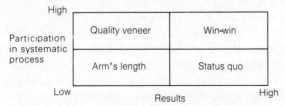

Figure 2 Executive board's role in PQI process.

Status quo.   The board wants to carry out its responsibilities but lacks the discipline to follow the structured approach of the systematic PQI process. Efforts are made in a random manner. Members might be heard saying, "I don't need to get involved with the details; that's what I pay my subordinates to do."

Typical outcome.   The results are generally mediocre. Although some may be outstanding, most fall short of expectations, and the process is not internalized or long-lasting.

Quality veneer.   Management adopts the jargon of PQI and does little to implement it or ineffectively implements it. More emphasis is placed on serving the system than working the system and the results it can provide. Very little support and encouragement are given to the teams.

Typical outcome.   Although the results occasionally meet expectations, the time to achieve them is excessively long. Charts are usually posted, but frequently with out-of-control points and indicating minimal improvement.

Win-win.   The executive board requires proper application of the systematic PQI process and executes its roles and responsibilities meticulously. It enthusiastically supports the teams, provides required resources, and rewards good performance.

Typical outcome.   Significant results are achieved according to expectations in terms of dollars and time. This mode provides more than survival; it sets the environment for a thriving level of growth.

Steering committee

The steering committee reports to the executive board. It directs and supports the activities of the teams implementing SPC. The steering committee consists principally of middle managers who are directly responsible for, or support, the processes being addressed. For a manufacturing steering committee the members are usually the quality engineering manager, the manufacturing engineering manager, the design engineering manager, and a finance manager. The leader of this committee, when addressing production processes, is most frequently the plant manager, manufacturing manager, or general manager. These managers usually have the most to gain from successful SPC and typically manage most of the resources to implement the program.

The steering committee oversees and enforces the policies set forth by the executive board. It establishes goals for productivity and quality improvement in an annual plan that are consistent with and supportive of the mission statement developed by the executive board. Members must have authority to change operating priorities, reallocate resources, reorganize teams, and support the teams without going through an encumbering approval process. This situation is ideal but there may be special cases (a minority of the decisions made) that require approval of the executive board. It performs these duties by

1. Coordinating input and developing the annual PQI plan (see Chap. 2)
2. Selecting projects and assigning priorities to them
3. Selecting team leaders and approving team members
4. Guiding teams through the 12-step process by
   a. providing direction, resources, and support
   b. approving closure of each step
   c. developing plans to recognize and reward performance
5. Conducting meetings to review team progress according to the milestone plan by
   a. resolving project constraint issues
   b. offering encouragement
   c. questioning constructively the team's logic and actions
   d. providing alternative solutions to problems
   e. appraising the performance of team leaders
6. Auditing the SPC implementation process on the manufacturing floor and project files
7. Reviewing proposals for additional projects
8. Scheduling and conducting quarterly project reviews with the executive board
9. Rewarding teams for their performance

In short, the steering committee must ensure the success of the project teams.

Project teams

An effective project team collectively has all necessary knowledge about the specific product or process in order to implement SPC. Team members are from design engineering, quality engineering, manufacturing engineering, quality control, production, and test engineering. Depending on the complexity or nature of the problem being addressed, representatives may be added from customer service, product development, supplier quality engineering, and receiving inspection.

The teams are guided by a team leader chosen, usually from first-level management, by the steering committee, and for the duration of the project team members report to and are directly accountable to the team leader on all phases of the project. For these activities, the individuals are primarily team members and secondarily representatives of their assigned functions. To avoid possible time conflicts between team activities and normal job functions, the steering committee must establish at the beginning of the program how much of each member's time should be spent supporting the team. Experience suggests an average of 10% of each member's time will allow for one hour of weekly meeting time and three hours for performing assignments. The project teams are responsible for executing the 12 steps of the PQI process. They must

1. Attend weekly meetings to review progress and coordinate future action

2. Identify obstacles to progress

3. Develop recovery plans to overcome obstacles

4. Communicate constraints to the steering committee when support is required, detailing the actual constraint, actions taken, and recommendations

5. Maintain documentation on each approved step

6. Identify and present future potential projects to the steering committee

In summary, the team is the final unit in the organizational structure having authority, power, and influence over the project. If the executive board and steering committee are fulfilling their responsibilities, then the project team is 100% accountable for the success or failure of its assigned project.

Team leader

The team leader manages the project team and is the most important individual in the process. The success of the program is typically directly proportional to the strength of the team leader. A good team leader, like a good manager, must have a balance of leadership, technical skills, and managerial skills. The leader may come from any department within the organization provided he or she is

- Results oriented
- Skilled at managing administrative details
- Skilled at managing time
- Able to create and sustain a climate of teamwork
- A skilled delegator, communicator, and motivator
- Skilled at leading group problem solving
- Skilled at coaching other team members
- Energetic enough to set the team's pace

The team leader must also be *biased for action*—in other words, a risk taker whose main approach is moving the team forward through planning and implementation.
The team leader

1. Helps choose team members
2. Schedules team meetings
3. Prepares meeting agenda
4. Assigns tasks to team members
5. Develops a preliminary milestone plane (see Chap. 2)
6. Issues weekly team progress reports
7. Identifies constraints, risks, and exposures and elevates any of these issues which the team cannot resolve to the steering committee for assistance
8. Develops recovery plans when applicable
9. Assures timely closure of each step of the 12-step PQI process
10. Evaluates members' performances and provides input to the appraisal process
11. Conducts presentations to the steering committee

The team leader has the most demanding job. He or she must be many things to many people. If the prospective team leader does not have all the requisite characteristics, the steering committee can choose someone on the basis of his or her future potential and develop that person in the deficient areas. This is one of the many side benefits that the process offers—it is also a vehicle for developing future leaders and managers.

Implementing with Teams

The team concept is not new. It has been used by businesses that had to introduce a critical program or project. The systematic PQI process presented in this book is not complex, and one individual *could* perform every step; however, individual contribution does not lead to rapid culture change. For this reason and to emphasize that productivity and quality improvement is everybody's business, businesses have preferred the team approach, and it has proven successful.

A *team* is two or more individuals who must coordinate their activities in pursuit of a common goal. This definition can help determine when the use of a team is appropriate. A team is most appropriate when

- Programs call for wide exposure in order to promote awareness throughout the organization
- A problem spans departmental boundaries
- Sequencing or coordination of effort is necessary to accomplish the proposed solution or goal
- Knowledge is needed from different specialists, or joint decisions are required
- No person has total control, influence, and authority over the problem, resources, or services
- No department has full ownership of the program
- Departmental barriers exist due to the company's culture operating in a traditional mode

The use of teams is especially effective because of the synergism created by the mixing of the members' various skills. *Synergism* is the simultaneous action of various elements, which together have a greater total effect than the sum of their individual contributions. For example, consider two people walking on train track rails. The first one walks 10 yards before falling off the rail, the second 15 yards before falling. However, when both walk together, one on each rail, while holding hands (teamwork) they are able to walk for miles.

Synergism is achieved in a team when an environment is created where

- The effectiveness of decision making is enhanced
- More innovative ideas are generated through group interaction
- The diverse talents and experiences of the members are best utilized
- The evaluations of the group will likely be more accurate assessments of situations
- Decisions made are generally supported by all parties included or affected
- Efforts of different specialists are effectively coordinated
- Team members and other managers often look at problems more deeply or objectively and reexamine their own biases and perspectives

The team concept is a powerful approach because of its ability to produce results as well as its educational contributions. In an effective team the potential of weaker, less experienced team members will be developed through their interactions with more experienced and knowledgeable members. Before beginning team activity, all members must be trained in the systematic 12-step PQI process so that they will understand and effectively carry out their responsibilities.

Role of the Facilitator

The facilitator is indispensable to the systematic PQI process. Broadly, the facilitator nurtures the development, leadership, and effectiveness of the team leader and team members and expedites the PQI process to obtain the best possible results. The facilitator must

- Be committed to the success of the project
- Be a recognized expert in SPC and experienced in introducing it to manufacturing operations (thus education, coaching, and advice will be positively received by anyone involved in the process)
- Be results oriented, with performance and tenure directly related to success
- Be intimately familiar with the 12-step PQI process
- Be a skilled motivator and coach
- Have technical knowledge and extensive background in manufacturing, service, or administration

The facilitator helps the team leader plan the project and organize the meetings, ensures that the outcome is clearly identified, sees to it that everyone participates, and maintains the integrity of the systematic process. The facilitator must educate, demonstrate, coach, and audit results of the SPC implementation (see Fig. 3). Effective facilitators are truly a rare breed.

The facilitator is

- A guide around the pitfalls and special applications not covered in textbooks

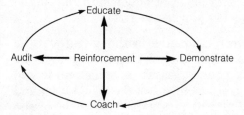

Figure 3 Role of facilitator illustrated as closed loop.

- A catalyst, providing follow-up to all management levels and thus maintaining continuity
- An objective evaluator and auditor of team progress, identifying any roadblocks to success

Specifically, the facilitator performs these responsibilities as follows:

1. Provides training and immediate applications of training
2. Modifies forms to meet project needs
3. Ensures that the team leader
   a. Documents each step
   b. Prepares a weekly progress report with an updated milestone plan
   c. Requests steering committee approval to modify systematic approach steps
   d. Submits to the steering committee adequate closure documentation for each step, IC and process capability studies reports, CP action matrix, and process control procedures
4. Recommends to the team leader (verbally) and to the advisor (verbally and in biweekly progress reports) solutions to disagreements about the project's direction, scope, and progress
5. Coaches team leaders before a meeting to have expected outcomes for the meeting and to limit the meeting to 1–1½ hours
6. Verbally critiques team leader's performance biweekly and works with him or her to overcome weaknesses, and gives written critiques to the advisor and to the chairperson of the steering committee
7. Conducts weekly audits of process control charts, CP action matrix, and events logs with supervisors and team leaders and makes suggestions for improvement
8. Reviews weekly the team leader's progress reports and critiques them for accuracy, concurrence, and compliance to the format
9. Reviews weekly the milestone plan for accuracy
10. Advises team leader of risks and exposures that the leader is unaware of and concurs with him or her on those risks and exposures; if facilitator does not concur, he or she must inform the advisor verbally and in biweekly progress reports

When using a facilitator, a person from either within or without the organization, the company must clarify the working arrangement by establishing mutually agreed upon guidelines. These guidelines should be consistent with the roles and responsibilities of the team leader and the facilitator. An effective facilitator is invaluable because he or she will see to it that everything is done right the first time. In the words of Robert Kleist, chief executive officer of Printronix, Inc., a leading

California computer printer manufacturer, "Doing it right the first time is the only way to increase profits."

Role of the Advisor

The advisor interacts with the steering committees and the president's executive board. The advisor must

- Provide guidance to the steering committee
- Guide the steering committee through steps and closure of steps on their initial pass
- Review presentations of team leaders by asking questions and providing suggestions
- Call for strategy sessions when required
- Observe behaviors in steering committee members and provide feedback to them
- Critique presentations of the team leader to president's quality executive board
- Critique performance of the steering committee chairperson

SUMMARY

In order for a company to successfully implement the PQI process, there must be a change in its culture that allows the improvements to be achieved and maintains the spirit and effort that led to the improvements. Thus it is critical that there be established within the company both an organization whose main elements are an executive board, a steering committee, and project teams; and a system for operating it that includes roles and responsibilities.

Once the organization is in place, strong team leaders and a strong steering committee chairperson must be selected for the specific projects. Then qualified team members are chosen. Finally, to provide guidance to the organization, an experienced facilitator and advisor are used.

Project Identification*

Project identification is step 1 of the PQI process. Projects are assigned to the project teams by the steering committee, but may be quite loosely defined because the steering committee has limited information when it makes assignments. Individuals or teams must then further define the project and develop an objective statement so that everyone involved with the process understands what is to be accomplished and agrees on the ultimate goal.

Products and processes targeted for implementation of SPC will be effective only if clearly identified at the beginning. The teams or individuals carry out this identification by defining in detail the magnitude of the problem being addressed, the potential savings, and the cost of implementing solutions to the problem.

If an assigned project is too broad for one team to handle effectively, it must be broken into elements or subprojects and given a set of priorities. The team then selects the most appropriate element to begin the process, and redefines and rejustifies the revised project to provide management sufficient information on the expected savings. From that information the steering committee determines if the project should receive more labor and resources.

The identification process is made easier and more thorough by a standard five-page form (Fig. 1.1) developed to assist teams in defining and financially justifying their projects. In addition to completing this form, the project team must create a process flow diagram. The entire package is then submitted for approval to the steering committee which action will satisfy the requirements for closure of step 1.

---

*Jack Dawson participated in preparing this chapter.

Project Definition

Responsible team _____

Project _____

I. Statement of problem

    A. Description:

        Part name _____   Part number(s) _____

        Model name _____   Model number _____

        Source plant _____   Customer plant _____

    B. Impact statement:

    C. Scope statement:

II. Summary of potential areas of improvement:

        Productivity improvement _____

        Quality improvement   _____

        Schedule improvement   _____

        Customer satisfaction   _____

        Estimated project duration (calendar weeks) _____

III. Required approvals

        Prepared by _____   _____

                      Team member   Date

        Approved by _____   _____

                      Team leader   Date

        Verified by _____   _____

                      Finance   Date

        Approved by _____   _____

                    Steering committee   Date

Figure 1.1 Project identification form.

Project Definition

Opportunities Checklist

	Applicable	
A. Productivity	Yes	No
Rework (labor): Source plant	___	___
Rework (labor): Customer plant	___	___
Manufacturing methods	___	___
Inspection techniques (labor)	___	___
Scrap (labor): Source plant	___	___
Amount of inspection (labor)	___	___
Reinspection (labor): Source plant	___	___
Reinspection (labor): Customer plant	___	___
B. Quality		
Critical operations	___	___
Scrap (material): Source plant	___	___
Scrap (material): Customer plant	___	___
Classification of characteristics	___	___
C. Schedule impact		
Variances	___	___
Shortage	___	___
Backlog	___	___
D. Customer satisfaction		
Customer installation quality	___	___
Customer reliability	___	___
Definition of rejects, including failure modes, locations, and time	___	___
Customer service response	___	___

Figure 1.1   *(Continued)*

Project Justification

Responsible team _____

Project _____

I. Performance history (past 3 months)

     Reject rate _____ Scrap rate _____

     Rework cost _____

     Production rate _____

     Schedule compliance _____

II. Worksheets summaries

Item	Potential annual savings	Identified annual savings	Implemen-tation cost	Return on investment [(column 2− col. 3) / col. 3]
Scrap (material)				
Rework (labor)				
Reinspection (labor)				
NCMRs				
Productivity				
Total				

III. Required approvals

     Prepared by: _____   _____
                        Team member   Date

     Approved by: _____   _____
                        Team leader   Date

     Verified by: _____   _____
                        Finance   Date

     Approved by: _____   _____
                      Steering committee   Date

Figure 1.1 *(Continued)*

Project Justification

Potential Annual Savings

A. Scrap

    (1) No. of pieces scrapped per month
    (2) Cost per piece scrapped   _____
    (3) Annual scrap cost [(1) x (2) x (12 months/yr)]   _____

B. Rework

    (1) No. of pieces reworked per month
    (2) Time (hrs) per piece to rework   _____
    (3) Cost per hr of repair person   _____
    (4) Annual rework cost [(1) x (2) x (3) x (12 months/yr)]   _____

C. Reinspection

    (1) No. of pieces reinspected per month
    (2) Time (hrs) per piece to reinspect   _____
    (3) Cost per hr of inspector   _____
    (4) Annual reinspection cost [(1) x (2) x (3) x (12 months/yr)]   _____

D. NCMRs or reject notices

    (1) No. of NCMRs per month
    (2) Average cost to process one NCMR   _____
    (3) Annual NCMR cost [(1) x (2) x (12 months/yr)]   _____

E. Productivity

    (1) No. of pieces per month
    (2) Time (hrs) per piece   _____
    (3) Cost per hr of labor   _____
    (4) Annual productivity cost [(1) x (2) x (3) x (12 months/yr)]   _____

Figure 1.1   (*Continued*)

Project Justification

F. Estimated productivity and quality improvements

Scrap	From ____ % to ____ % or ____ % improvement
Rework	From ____ % to ____ % or ____ % improvement
Reinspection	From ____ % to ____ % or ____ % improvement
NCMRs	From ____ % to ____ % or ____ % improvement
Productivity	From ____ % to ____ % or ____ % improvement

G. Identified annual savings

	(1)	(2)	(3)
(A) Scrap (material)	= $ _____	x _____	= $ _____
(B) Rework (labor)	= $ _____	x _____	= $ _____
(C) Reinspection (labor)	= $ _____	x _____	= $ _____
(D) NCMRs	= $ _____	x _____	= $ _____
(E) Productivity	= $ _____	x _____	= $ _____

H. Implementation cost

(1) Cost of new tools (special)   _____

(2) Cost of new equipment (machinery)   _____

(3) Cost of new supplies   _____

                                  Total   _____

Figure 1.1   *(Continued)*

In this chapter we discuss the elements of project identification—the definition statement, the project definition and justification form, and the process flow diagram—using the sample form in Fig. 1.1.

The Definition Statement

During the formative phase of the project, a problem or opportunity is presented to the project team by the steering committee with proposals for improved performance. The team must now clearly define the problem and the objective. The definition will be on the attached forms and will be used to make the objective statement for the project. The objective statement should be documented and will appear as the first item on each weekly progress report issued by the team. It must be specific, agreed upon, attainable, quantifiable, and time bounded. Examples of clear objective statements are, Reduce the percent defective on XY component from 5 to 2% by January 1, 1987, or, Increase the yield on ABC process from 85 to 97% by July 1, 1987, and to 99% by November 1, 1987.

The objective statement is important because it is the foundation on which the team will justify the project, formulate the action plan, and utilize precious resources to solve problems. It is the team's guiding light for focusing its efforts. A poorly defined or vague objective produces frustration, anxiety, waste of resources and time, loss of momentum, and disillusionment in the process; and the expected results will never occur.

Project Definition and Justification Form

Project definition

The first two pages of the form allow the team to define and document the project by a statement of the problem, a short summary of potential areas of improvement, and an area to formally obtain the required approvals.

Section I on page 1 begins with the statement of the problem and requires complete information of the description, impact, and scope of the project. The description is a list of the affected components or processes, including the names and part numbers of rejected components, the processes involved in making these components, and the places where the components are used. For example: Aluminum cross-flow radiator, part number 551386, vacuum braze process, plant 10, building 8, used on the Corvette 302 engine only.

The impact statement is a general statement of the effect of the problem, such as low yields or schedule constraints due to scrap and rework.

For example: 15 repaired radiators per 100 assemblies brazed, 15% defective, or 60 late orders per week. The dollar value and the problem impact are always included if sufficient information is available: for example, $5000 per week rework cost.

The scope statement defines where the problem is occurring (afternoon shift, or two of five machines), the plant location (fabrication department), geographic location (East or West Coast), or field location.

Section II on page 1 is a short summary of possible gains in productivity, quality, scheduling, and customer satisfaction—the result of successfully solving the problem. It is actually a distillation of the opportunities checklist (page 2 of the form). The estimated project duration is the team's best estimate of the time it will take to complete the 12-step PQI process.

The opportunities checklist details the many areas within the scope of a manufacturing organization that might be contributing to a particular problem. The intent of this list is to cause the team to think about how the problem may affect productivity, quality, scheduling, and customer satisfaction. Teams should review the checklist for potential savings in those areas and are encouraged to add new opportunities if they are identified. The checklist is divided into four categories:

1. *Productivity.* The team should identify any opportunities in productivity improvements that are related to labor, including manufacturing methods and inspection techniques (100% or sampling). Operations causing scrap or rework normally require reinspection; therefore they represent opportunities for labor reduction. The team should also review current manufacturing and inspection methods (if available) for completeness and accuracy.

2. *Quality.* Opportunities related to quality are concerned with scrap material or rework and range from external supplier or internal source to the customer. The customer may be an internal customer or the end user. The quality and process engineering departments are sometimes limited in their knowledge of the original design requirements or final use of the product. Product engineering must identify the critical characteristics of the product, including dimensions and operations. Quality and process engineering will then definitely check at least those characteristics considered critical to the function or assembly of the components, and cut back on inspecting dimensions considered noncritical. In some operations the inspection stations may be improperly placed.

3. *Schedule impact.* Opportunities in schedule impact will be identified by the impact that a source department (internal supplier) will have on another department (customer) in meeting schedules, includ-

ing time lost due to rescheduling, additional setups, or idle time because of a shortage within manufacturing.

4. *Customer satisfaction.* Customer satisfaction identifies opportunities related to the processes and adds statements from internal customers and final customers, such as poor installation quality, inadequate service response, or failure to meet reliability targets. Customer responses should be reviewed for definitions of rejects, failure modes, locations, and time of failures. Once the internal opportunities are identified, the internal customers can be interviewed to verify that the opportunities are valid. Any new information gained from these interviews should be added to the checklist. If possible, it is also beneficial to interview a sample of the final customers. This will close the loop for all possibilities and verify those opportunities that have been identified.

Project justification

Project justification is the second section of the form. These three pages are worksheets used by the team to determine the annual savings for each project. The team estimates the annual cost in dollars of the problem, annual savings potential, cost to implement the improvements, and return on investment for the project.

Before diving into the estimate calculations, the team must indicate the performance history (Section I, page 3). The performance history is a brief summary of the process performance for the past three months in terms of reject and scrap rates, productivity, rework, and schedule compliance. The team then annualizes the three-month performance rate over 12 months. This establishes a reference for measuring future improvements.

Section II, page 3, is a summary of the calculations brought forward from the worksheets on pages 4 and 5. The potential annual savings (column 1) is the annualized cost actually experienced. In other words, it is the savings that would be realized if 100% of the potential were achieved. For example, if scrap were reduced from 6 to 0%, the potential annual savings would be the dollar value of 6% annual scrap.

The identified annual savings (column 2) are numbers carried forward from Section G, page 5. These numbers represent the financial goals of the project team.

Implementing SPC does not usually require additional direct labor hours or capital expenditures to achieve the objectives. However, if such expenditures are required (e.g., improved or new equipment to meet specifications), the team must calculate the implementation cost by totaling all equipment costs, including new machine or tool designs. These costs are totaled in Section H on page 5 and entered in the "Total" row in column 3 of Section II on page 3. In a few projects the problems encountered while installing SPC and the implementation cost are not known until the problem analysis step (step 4 of the PQI process) is completed. In this case it is acceptable to complete the savings analysis being performed here with the information available. This analysis must then be revised and resubmitted for approval when the missing costs have been determined.

Return on investment (column 4) is determined as follows:

$$(\text{Column } 2 - \text{Column } 3)/\text{Column } 3 = \text{Column } 4$$

The ratio for an acceptable return on investment may vary from 4:1 to 10:1 depending on the policy established by the steering committee.

Sections A through E on page 4 are straightforward calculations of cost that are transformed into annualized potential savings. These figures are carried to column 1 of Section G (page 5) and to column 1 of Section II (page 3). Savings involving labor are calculated by the direct labor rate plus an estimated 20% for fringe benefits (or actual rate if it is available from the cost accounting department).

Section F asks the team to estimate the productivity and quality improvements in terms of percent improvement. This is done for each area or category that the team previously identified as an opportunity. The team reviews the current rate (percent) and estimates the final rate (or objective target) that it believes will result from successfully applying the 12-step process to this project and resolving other problems that might be encountered. For example, reducing a scrap rate from 6 to 2% gives a 66.7% improvement. The calculation is done as follows:

$$\frac{6\% - 2\%}{6\%} \times 100 = 66.7\%$$

These percentages are then carried to column 2 of Section G. Multiplying columns 1 and 2 of Section G gives column 3. The numbers in column 3 are entered in column 2 of Section II (page 3).

If the actual information for calculating the numbers on the form is unavailable, then the team must use its best estimates of available information. A detailed financial analysis is *not* required and would only serve to stall the team's progress. The purpose of this step is to quickly determine if the project is worth the team's effort and resources and to translate the objective targets into real dollar goals. (We show in Chaps. 2 and 12 how the actual performance and results are measured for effectiveness.) The team should, however, ask that the finance department review the preliminary estimates. A finance representative's signature on page 1 of the form indicates that in the representative's opinion the numbers are reasonable and no significant errors or incorrect assumptions were made.

Process Flow Diagram

The third element in the project identification step is the preparation of a process flow diagram for the process being addressed. This diagram helps the team to determine the critical operations and to pinpoint where process control charts will be most applicable and effective. A flow diagram shows the processes that collectively or sequentially produce the final product. (A *process* can be defined as any combination of materials, machines, tools, methods, and people that create through specifications the desired products or services.) Processes are found in manufacturing, service, and support operations. Support processes are typically found in office or administrative operations. The flow diagram also establishes the boundaries in which the team must confine its project involvement. Steering committees, anxious to see results, may occasionally make assignments not relative to implementing SPC within the defined project. Teams also may tend to sidetrack and want to investigate an interesting but unrelated potential opportunity. The combination of a clear objective and a process flow diagram focuses the activities of the team within the originally defined project.

The team should determine if a process flow diagram exists and if so, review it for accuracy and completeness. To review the flow diagram or to prepare one, the team should visit the location(s) where the process is being performed, observe the activities, and interview the key people in the process. While reviewing the process, the team should pay particular attention to the items or characteristics checked at each inspection point.

A flow diagram is constructed with symbols that represent various operations or processes. Figure 1.2 shows suggested symbols for constructing a manufacturing flow diagram. Figure 1.3 shows how the symbols are used. Figure 1.4 is a complete flow diagram for assembling printed circuit boards.

The actual symbols in a flow diagram are not as important as ensuring that all key operations or processes are identified on the diagram and that they are understood. A standard set of symbols eliminates confusion from diagram to diagram.

SUMMARY

After the project team completes the objective statement, project definition and justification form, and process flow diagram, it submits the

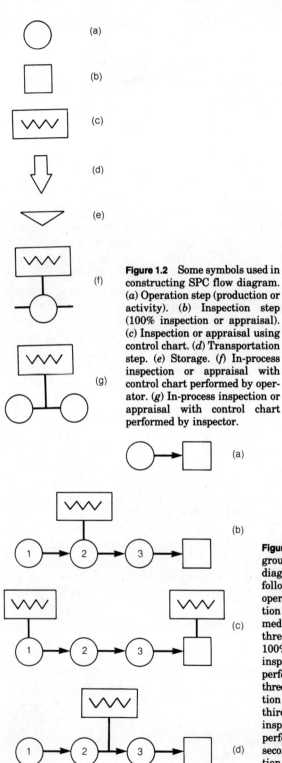

Figure 1.2 Some symbols used in constructing SPC flow diagram. (*a*) Operation step (production or activity). (*b*) Inspection step (100% inspection or appraisal). (*c*) Inspection or appraisal using control chart. (*d*) Transportation step. (*e*) Storage. (*f*) In-process inspection or appraisal with control chart performed by operator. (*g*) In-process inspection or appraisal with control chart performed by inspector.

Figure 1.3 Some examples of groups of symbols in SPC flow diagrams. (*a*) Single operation followed by 100% inspection operation. (*b*) In-process inspection with control chart performed by operator at second of three operations followed by 100% inspection. (*c*) In-process inspection with control chart performed by operator at first of three operations with 100% inspection with control chart after third operation. (*d*) In-process inspection with control chart performed by inspector after second process with 100% inspection after third operation.

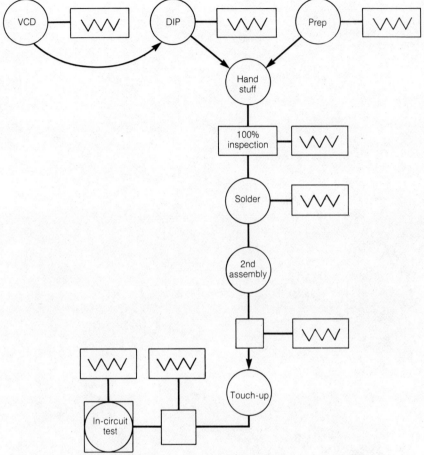

Figure 1.4 Printed circuit board assembly flow diagram. VCD stands for variable component device machine, DIP for dual in-line package machine.

package to the steering committee for approval. This not only allows the team to close step 1, but it also informs the steering committee about the magnitude of the problem and provides a base for deciding whether to proceed with the project.

2

Planning and Reporting*

A well-conceived plan and a comprehensive progress report are essential ingredients for the success of any project. In the last chapter the project team carefully defined and cost justified its project and had it approved by the steering committee. The team must now quickly move ahead to step 2 of the systematic process, planning and reporting. This chapter provides detailed guidelines and a format for

- Documenting each step of the systematic 12-step process on a milestone plan

- Submitting project team progress reports and steering committee progress reports

- Presenting formal quarterly status reports to the executive committee

- Developing the annual PQI plan

The team must establish a project plan at this stage of the process so that for the duration of the project the members will maximize their time and efforts and maintain the focus and direction of activities. The plan also establishes goals for completing each step of the PQI process. Likewise, a periodic progress report not only helps the team leader manage the project, but it keeps team members focused on project assignments and keeps the steering committee and executive committee informed about the team's progress.

---

*Jack Dawson participated in preparing this chapter.

The Milestone Plan

Industry requires a plan for successful projects where teams solve problems that might save thousands of dollars. In the 12-step PQI process this plan is called a *milestone plan*. It lists the 12 steps of the process together with their corresponding start and completion dates. Each step of the process is a "milestone," and completing a milestone is a major accomplishment of the team. The milestone plan is used by the team to stay on track and by the steering committee to monitor the progress of the team's project.

A blank milestone plan form is shown in Fig. 2.1. The team chooses start and completion dates for each step. All dates on the milestone plan correspond to Friday of each week. The duration of each step is shown by an S in the column under the appropriate starting date and a C under the appropriate completion date. The S and C are then connected with a dashed line like this: S– – –C.

After starting or completing a step, the team should update the milestone plan with the *actual* dates by adding parentheses around the S or C. The milestone plan is a flexible tool and recognizes that circumstances may require rescheduling some of the steps. Reschedules are indicated with RS (rescheduled start) and RC (rescheduled completion). The percent completed should also be indicated with asterisks on the plan for steps in progress:

$$S{***}(RS){*****}C{**}\text{– – – }RC \qquad 75\%$$

As a guideline, the average project should be completed within three months. The initial plan is submitted to and approved by the steering committee. Then each team progress report should include the milestone plan with its current status. A completed milestone plan is shown in Fig. 2.2.

Project Progress Reporting

Team progress report

The 12-step process requires a progress report after every team meeting. The report is structured primarily to assist the team leader to manage the project and to communicate progress to the readers. A specific report format must be used to minimize preparation time and maximize the amount of useful information it contains.

Each progress report includes project objectives, status, accomplishments, exceptions to plan, risks and exposures, outlook, detailed assignments, milestone plan, and performance measurements (see Chap. 3). The general format of the team progress report is shown in Fig. 2.3. A completed example is shown in Fig. 2.4.

Milestone Plan

Project: Prepared by:

Objective: Date issued:

Legend: Date revised:

Legend		
S Planned start	RS Rescheduled start	(S) Actual start
C Planned completion	RC Rescheduled completion	(C) Actual completion
• Percent completed	N/A Not applicable	

Dates

Milestone
1. Project identification
Definition
Justification
Flow diagram
2. Planning and reporting
Milestone plan and progress report
3. Performance measurements
Productivity and quality
4. Problem analysis and solution
Events log
Cause and effect diagram
5. Inspection capability
Plan
Study
6. Process capability
Plan
Study
7. Corrective and preventive action matrix
8. Process control procedure
9. Process control implementation
10. Problem prevention
11. Defect accountability
12. Measurement of effectiveness
Process audit
Product audit
Systems audit
Financial audit

Figure 2.1 Milestone plan form.

Milestone Plan

Project: Gold plating
Objective: Reduce rework from 20 to 5%

Prepared by: S. Alm
Date issued:
Date revised: 1/10/83

Legend:
S   Planned start
C   Planned completion
•   Percent completed

RS Rescheduled start
RC Rescheduled completion
N/A Not applicable

(S) Actual start
(C) Actual completion

Dates

Milestone	Nov. 22 29	Dec. 6 13 20 27	Jan. 3 10 17 24 31	Feb. 7 14 21 28
1. Project identification				
Definition	(S)•••(C)	100%		
Justification	(S)•••(C)	100%		
Flow diagram	(S)••••(C)	100%		
2. Planning and reporting				
Milestone plan and progress report	(S)•••••••(C)	100%		
3. Performance measurements				
Productivity and quality	S•••••(S)•••••••••(C) 100%			
4. Problem analysis and solution				
Events log		(S)•••••••(C)		
Cause and effect diagram		(S)•••••••(C)		
5. Inspection capability		S•••••••••••(C)		
Plan				
Study				
6. Process capability		(S)•••C•• RC		
Plan				
Study				
7. Corrective and preventive action matrix				
8. Process control procedure		(S)•--C RC		
9. Process control implementation				
10. Problem prevention				S----C
11. Defect accountability				S------C
12. Measurement of effectiveness				
Process audit			S----C	
Product audit				S----C
Systems audit				
Financial audit				

Figure 2.2 Milestone plan example.

Project objectives. The objective should include a general statement about the project. Performance targets should be identified relative to time and performance measurement indicators, such as percent defective. All targets and indicators should be quantified and converted to dollars wherever possible. Information about the objective of the team in terms of percent improvement and dollars to be saved has already been determined in step 1, project identification (Chap. 1). The objective will not change from week to week and might be stated on the progress report like this:

Decrease the number of PCBs reworked at gold plating

Current	Goal	Cost Savings
20%	5%	$420,000

To: Team members, steering committee members, and team members' managers
From: Team leader
Subject: Team progress report
Date:
Team members
*Absent

   I. Project objectives
     A. Statement
     B. Quantified target
  II. Status
     A. Steps completed
     B. Steps in process
     C. Performance to objective
     D. Major problems identified
     E. Actions taken and planned
 III. Accomplishments
     A. In-process steps completed
     B. Assignments completed
 IV. Exceptions to plan
     A. Statement of problem
     B. Recovery plan
  V. Risks and exposures
     A. Identified constraints
     B. Causes of constraints
     C. Recommended action
 VI. Outlook
     A. Completion date of current step
     B. Overall project completion date
     C. Projected value of savings and performance
VII. Detailed assignments
     A. Activity
     B. Responsible team member
     C. Target date
     D. Status
VIII. Milestone plan
 IX. Performance measurements
     A. Quality indicator
     B. Productivity indicator
     C. Money saved

Figure 2.3 General format of team progress report.

Milestone Plan

Project: Gold plating
Objective: Reduce rework from 20 to 5%

Legend:
S   Planned start
C   Planned completion
•   Percent completed

RS   Rescheduled start
RC   Rescheduled completion
NA   Not applicable

(S)   Actual start
(C)   Actual completion

Approved by: M. Schnell
Date issued: 12/16/83
Date revised: 8/9/84

Dates

Milestone	Apr. 6 13 20 27	May 4 11 18 25	June 1 8 15 22 29	July 6 13 20 27	Aug. 6 13 20 27
1. Project identification					
Definition	(S)····(C)				
Justification	(S)····(C)				
Flow diagram		(S)·······(C)			
2. Planning and reporting					
Milestone plan and progress report		(S)··········(C)			
3. Performance measurements					
Productivity and quality		S······· (S)······(C)	100%		
4. Problem analysis and solution					
Events log			(S)···············(C)		
Cause and effect diagram			(S)···············(C)		
5. Inspection capability		S···············(C)			
Plan					
Study			(S)··········C········- RC		
6. Process capability					
Plan					
Study					
7. Corrective and preventive action matrix					
8. Process control procedure			(S)·····-C	RC	
9. Process control implementation					
10. Problem prevention				S-----C	
11. Defect accountability				S-----C	
12. Measurement of effectiveness					
Process audit			S-----------C		
Product audit					S-----C
Systems audit					
Financial audit					

100%
100%
100%
100%

Figure 2.4   Team progress report example.

To: Distribution   Date: August 10
From: M. Schultz
Subject: Productivity and quality improvement process team—gold plating meeting held each
         Monday at 1 p.m., Plant 1, Training Room.
Team members

J. Carlson	Quality Engineer
H. Crespy	Inspection
R. Sizemore	Manufacturing Engineer
D. Dortman*	Production Supervisor
M. George	Production Operator
C. Moore	Test
W. Manning	Facilitator
M. Schultz	Team Leader

*Absent

I. Project objective
   A. Decrease the number of PCBs reworked at gold plating.

Current	Goal	Cost Savings
20%	5%	$420,000

II. Status
    A. Steps completed.
       1. Steps 1 through 6 of the 12-step process are complete.
    B. Steps in process.
       1. Step 7, CP action matrix, is being developed by the team for gold plating.
    C. Performance to objective.

Actual	Goal
8%	5%

    D. Major problems identified.
       1. The timer for recording amperage on the plating tank was broken on the second shift.
          a. Recovery plan: John Williams will contact maintenance to have it replaced and
             calibrated.
          b. Target date: Jan. 11 for installation.
          c. Follow-up: Jan. 12 by M. Schultz.
III. Accomplishments
     A. In-process steps completed.
        1. Step 6, process capability study, was completed for gold plating and found to be
           unacceptable: Rick Sizemore.
     B. Assignments completed.
        1. None
IV. Exceptions to plan
    A. Statement of problem.
       1. The gold plating process is not in statistical process control; therefore, the completion
          date must be rescheduled.
    B. Recovery plan.
       1. Develop a design of experiments to determine the cause of the variation.
       2. Responsibility: R. Sizemore.
       3. Target date: Jan. 18.
    C. Inspection capability study has not been published; it has been delinquent since 7/30/84.
       Responsibility: Jim Carlson.
V. Risks and exposures
   A. None
   B. Action plan

Figure 2.4 *(Continued)*

VI. Outlook
  A. Step 11, defect accountability, will be completed on August 15.
  B. Expect project completion on September 27.
  C. The outlook is favorable; the team will meet the goal of $420,000 savings.
VII. Detailed assignments

Activity	Responsibility	Status due date	Follow-up date
1. Evaluate process capability study	Team	8/27	
2. Publish inspection capability study	J. Carlson	7/30 8/7 (rescheduled)	
	B. Taylor	8/21	
3. Develop CP action matrix	Team	8/27	

Distribution:
Team members
Team members' managers
Steering committee members

Figure 2.4 (*Continued*)

Status. The status section has four subsections. The first is a statement of how many steps of the 12-step process are completed. The second is a statement of which steps of the 12-step process are in process. The third is a statement of current project performance versus the stated objective. The last section lists specific problems being addressed and the progress toward their resolution. Information including the individuals assigned to the problem, the action being taken, and a target date for completion of the action should be listed in the detailed assignments section of the report.

Accomplishments. The accomplishments section is a statement of assignments completed since the last report. Accomplishments mentioned on previous reports need not be repeated. The steps, if any, that have been completed and any other significant accomplishments should be included. We strongly recommended that those responsible for completed assignments be mentioned by name and given special recognition. This section is not an activities list, so only accomplishments that contributed to the successful completion of the step should be mentioned.

Exceptions to plan. Exceptions to plan describes steps that are not on schedule according to the approved milestone plan, or whose scope has changed for any reason, or those assignments that had an inadequate response or result. A recovery plan is required to bring the project back on schedule. The recovery plan must include the planned action, the person responsible for taking the action, a target date for completion of the planned action, and a date for follow-up by the team leader or supervisor of the planned action.

Risks and exposures.   Risks and exposures identifies constraints that may prevent the team from successfully closing any step or assignment. This section acts like a relief valve for the team and is an effective means to alert management that its support is needed. However, no risk should be brought to the attention of the steering committee unless the team has first tried to solve the problem. If the team is unsuccessful, the problem should be brought to the attention of management for action or support. The team leader must indicate the causes of the constraints along with a status of action the team has taken and a recommended action plan. The causes should identify missed target dates and the responsible individuals, adverse budget performance, and any other performance shortfalls. The recommended action plan to offset the constraints should identify responsible individuals and the target dates for completion.

Outlook.   The outlook forecasts the team's projection in terms of dates and performance for the outcome of the project. The anticipated completion dates should be stated for the step in progress and for the project as a whole. A statement should also be made regarding the expected *performance* of the project versus the objective. Any exceptions to plan, including appropriate recovery plans, should be noted.

Detailed assignments.   On a separate page each weekly assignment should be listed, including actions assigned, individuals responsible, dates for completing the assignments, and follow-up work. Assignments completed on time are listed for one week as "completed" and then dropped from the report. Assignments not completed on time must be rescheduled with new target dates. Dates for follow-up by team leaders or supervisors to ensure completion of the assignments must also be scheduled. The rescheduled target date is listed below the original target date. Any assignment not completed by the second scheduled date requires the attention of the steering committee, which then reassigns the work to the manager of the delinquent team member for completion.

   Publishing the team progress report is the responsibility of the team leader. The progress report is based on the minutes of the team meeting and must be issued within 24 hours of the meeting. The report reminds team members of their assignments. The report is distributed to all team members, their managers or supervisors, and members of the steering committee. All team members are listed on the progress report, and any member absent from a scheduled meeting has an asterisk next to his or her name. The team progress report also serves as the agenda for the next team and steering committee meetings, where each section should be thoroughly reviewed.

Steering committee progress report

The steering committee progress report highlights the project status and assignments for the executive board, provides feedback to the teams on the resolution of risk and exposure items, and states activities planned by the steering committee. This report must be in writing and is issued by the chair of the steering committee to the vice presidents and team leaders within 24 hours of the steering committee meeting. The report format should include status, accomplishments, assignments, and planned activities. A completed example is shown in Fig. 2.5.

Status. In the status section of the report all team projects that were reviewed that week are identified. Included is the progress of each team relative to its milestone plan, each team's current performance compared to the stated objective, and the outlook for project completion. Progress made by a team relative to the corporate annual PQI plan is also listed in this section.

Accomplishments. The first part of the next section states team accomplishments. The steering committee's accomplishments are listed in the second part and includes resolution of problems related to risks and exposures and exceptions to plan.

Assignments. The next section describes any assignments of steering committee members, such as activities to address resolution of risks and exposures and exceptions to plan, in support of the teams.

Planned activities. Planned activities include the date, time, and location of the next meeting and a list of teams to be reviewed at that meeting. Special publications, meetings, and a schedule of projects from the annual PQI plan may also be indicated.

Quarterly Presentations

Once each quarter the steering committee chairperson schedules formal presentations to the executive committee. All team members attend to support the team leader, who makes the presentation, which is basically a summary of the weekly team progress reports. The elements of the presentation are

To: Distribution   Date: August 17

From: Lyle Aikens   Reference: Meeting held August 16

Subject: Plant 1 PQI steering committee meeting minutes

I. Status
  A. Reviewed the progress of PCB gold plating team. Inspection capability study complete. Process capability study is on target for completion on 8/17. The team is on target for a mid-September completion.
  B. The axial DIP team reviewed the process capability study and resolved the concern over the operator's prescreening PCBs during the study. It was agreed to leave the current control limits in place; the operator will prescreen for defects. However, the inspector will pull every fifth board whether or not the operator spots a problem on it and perform normal inspection.
  C. The PCB test team resolved issues on the ATE equipment and completed the process capability study. The team will proceed to evaluate the 200 rejects from plant 2.

II. Accomplishments
  A. Clarified direction in PCB team.
  B. Restructured steering committee attendance for plants 1 and 2.

III. Assignments
  A. All team leaders:
    1. Determine status with quality engineering PQI team files.
    2. Record attendance on weekly minutes.
  B. Team leaders bring PQI team files to their respective steering committee meetings and report status.
  C. Formulate a plan for the teams' use of plant 1 engineering support resources. Put up charts of plant 1 reject data in plant 2 subtest area.
  D. Release axial DIP process control procedure through manufacturing engineering (S. Manley).
  E. Discussion on proposals for a benefit system (8/23).
  F. Restructure steering committee and guests for plants 1 and 2 (L. Kent, B. Bonwell—complete).

IV. Planned activities
  A. Next meeting scheduled for Thursday, August 23, in the plant 2 training room at 10 a.m.
  B. Topics
    1. Hour 1: Review status of
      a. Kit staging (Dool).
      b. Solder coating (Pratt).
      c. Chrome process (Kennedy).
    2. Hour 2: General review (steering committee)
      a. L. Kent, B. Bonwell, S. Samuels, F. Johnson, D. Newsome.

Distribution:
Team leaders
Steering committee members

Figure 2.5 Steering committee progress report example.

- Team objective
- Steps completed and in process
- Performance measurements (current versus objective)
- Accomplishments
- Exceptions to plan with recovery plan
- Risks and exposures with action plan
- Outlook performance and project completion

Annual Productivity and Quality Improvement Plan

Date _____

Product line _____

Priority	Project and objective description	Projected annual savings	Productivity or quality measurement	Target milestone plan	
				Year _____ Q1 Q2 Q3 Q4	Year _____ Q1 Q2 Q3 Q4

Figure 2.6 Annual PQI plan form.

Annual PQI Plan

The annual PQI plan provides a format to list and plan all potential opportunities for future productivity and quality improvements. Input to the plan comes from the project teams and the steering committee. The plan is summarized by the steering committee for presentation to the executive committee at the quarterly meeting.

The plan specifically lists potential projects that have been defined to the extent described in step 1 (Chap. 1). That is, it has a specific objective stated in terms of percent or level of improvement and the associated annualized savings that can be realized. It also has recommended target and completion dates, with responsible individuals or teams identified whenever possible. A recommended format is displayed in Fig. 2.6.

The input comes primarily from project teams as they uncover problems or opportunities that are beyond the scope of their current project. To make sure the plan is a realistic working document, the team should perform the preliminary identification and justification activities and state them in potential dollar savings. Information from the individual team plans is then presented to the executive committee, which should review and incorporate the plans into its annual operating plan with the same level of certainty as the annual production and sales plans. The teams should review and update their plans at least monthly and before meeting with the executive committee.

SUMMARY

The project team may close step 2 when the milestone plan has been completed and approved, progress reporting has begun, and the annual PQI plan format is established. Armed with a plan of attack for its project and a vehicle for reporting its progress, the team is ready to move on to step 3, performance measurements, where it will determine the criteria and system for actually measuring the progress and performance of its project.

Performance Measurements*

At this stage in the PQI process the team has already clearly identified the project and calculated a preliminary justification that indicates potential for substantial improvement. Successful completion of the project will generate returns to justify the expenditure of worker-hours and resources. Thus the team and steering committee have agreed to continue with the project, weekly team meetings have begun, and progress reporting of the project has started.

In Chap. 1 a problem or opportunity for improvement was brought into focus. At that point the team established a reference base for measurement of improvement. The objective may have been stated in terms such as, reduce percent defective from 10 to 2%, or increase yield from 85 to 98%, or increase productivity from 65 to 98%. The target objective was defined in specific measurable terms. Now a system must be established to measure, record, and report performance against that objective as viewed by the internal customer or end customer.

Performance measurement is step 3 in the PQI process. Performance measurements indicate the effectiveness of the team's efforts by demonstrating in objective terms (1) the current status versus the target objective, and (2) the progress over time toward achieving that target. The actions for developing performance measurements are

1. Determine the measurement criteria
2. Establish a measurement system

---

*Thomas Zimmerman participated in preparing this chapter.

3. Collect the data

4. Report the performance

Determine the Measurement Criteria

Being measurable is not always sufficient. Criteria such as percent defective or yield are usually easy to quantify and measure. On the other hand, measurement of cost of quality, for example, is considerably more complex and may involve virtually every facet of a company. Therefore, before a measurement system is implemented, the project team must be sure that the objective is measurable and within the scope of the team to measure and report. The team may need to divide the target objective into specific elements of the main objective. Take, for example, the objective to increase productivity of ALPHA printed circuit boards (which contain BETA resistors) from 80 to 95% by 1/1/87. This may be divided into two, more specific, objectives with individual measurement systems that support the main objective:

1. Increase yield of ALPHA printed-circuit-board testing from 85 to 98% by 11/1/86.

2. Reduce percent defective of BETA resistors from 25 to 5% by 10/1/86

Some typical examples of performance measurements for manufacturing operations are listed in Table 3.1. The list is certainly not exhaustive and is provided only as a starting point and memory jogger. A frequently used system measuring productivity complies with the following definitions:

Productivity = Percentage indicator that measures the output (earned hours) versus input (available hours)

$$= \frac{\text{Earned hours}}{\text{Available hours}} \times 100\%$$

Specific contributors to productivity are

Utilization = Percentage indicator measuring the amount of time an operator was used to produce the product versus the total hours worked

$$= \frac{\text{Actual hours}}{\text{Available hours}} \times 100\%$$

Efficiency = Percentage indicator measuring an operator's performance on an operation

$$= \frac{\text{Earned hours}}{\text{Actual hours}} \times 100\%$$

TABLE 3.1 Performance Measurements

Schedule	Productivity	Cost	Quality
Yield	Percent efficiency	Cost savings and reduction	Percent defective
Variance	Percent utilization	Profit improvement	Rework
Pieces per hour	Percent productivity	Cost avoidance	Scrap
Units per day		Inventory	Defects or errors per unit or hundred
Shortages		Rework (material and labor)	Weighting defects (demerits)
Backlog		Scrap	Inspector and appraiser effectiveness
Lots processed		Labor efficiency	Percent error-free
Average days throughout		Materials	Cost of quality
Lots rejected			Incoming quality
Volume			
Forecast			
Mix			
Build plan			
Percent lots accepted			
Errors per opportunity			

where

Earned hours

Actual hours

Available hours

Standard hours

Hours earned by producing acceptable product as measured by inspection and multiplied by the labor standard (hr/unit): quantity accepted × standard hours

Direct labor hours or time spent producing the product, including normal rework

Total direct labor hours available for manufacturing, including time such as downtime, training, meetings, and abnormal rework, but not including vacation, absenteeism, holidays, tardiness, or leaving early

A predetermined time per unit used in generating a fixed cost standard and in establishing an operator's standard of performance

Other measurements, such as pieces per day or units per hour, may be used until productivity, utilization, and efficiency measures become available. The quality measurements listed in the table relate to the quality of a manufacturing operation, a test operation, or inspection leakages at a quality control operation. They are usually stated in terms of percent defective, percent defect free, defects per unit, or percent rejected.

An important principle applies at this point: The number or quantity of items produced must be *acceptable* product, not just "built" product. The team must keep this concept in mind when determining the measurement criteria and reporting the results.

The measurement criteria that the team selects will be based on the particular project or operation, specifically, the objective statement. Since the original project objective was justified in terms of dollars, the final criterion for selecting a performance measurement is that it must also relate to cost in dollars. If it is not a direct or obvious relationship, such as reduce scrap expense by 10%, then it must be capable of being translated into dollars. Therefore, the team should work closely with the finance and cost accounting departments during steps 1 and 3 in the PQI process.

Establish a Measurement System

Now that the measurement criteria have been selected, the team must establish a measurement system. The team has already decided *what* will be measured; it must now determine *how* it will be measured. The important factors to consider are

1. Responsibility for the system
2. Cost versus complexity
3. Timeliness of information

At least one member of the project team should be assigned the responsibility for the performance measurement system. That person will see to it that the system is implemented and that the data are collected and reported on schedule. This responsibility may not entail the actual doing, but it does call for the person to coordinate the activities of team members who are representatives of different departments and organizations. If the performance being measured is in the functional area of a team member, then that member is the logical choice to assume this responsibility.

Project teams often find that the information they need is already available in one form or another in the company's reporting system. It may then only be a matter of extracting data, reformatting a report, or performing simple reprogramming of a current report to sort the information differently. Ideally, the team will use a computer system to do the work for it. If that is not available, then a decision must be made as to the value of an investment in such a system versus data generation by hand. That same decision must also include consideration of the timeliness of performance reporting. Hand-generated data, though perhaps less expensive now, if not readily available may be a roadblock to the team rather than a tool for analysis or an indicator when action is required.

The team must take care not to select measurements or systems "in a vacuum" and should be aware of performance interrelationships. If there is the possibility of a tradeoff between critical parameters, then the team should implement measurement systems and monitor performance in all of the affected areas. For example, an increase in productivity might result in a decrease in quality, so both parameters should be monitored.

Collect the Data

When establishing the measurement system, the team must consider who collects the data, how frequently data are collected, in what format data should appear, and what happens to the data after they are collected. Determining who collects the information depends on the type of data and the system used. In this regard the most important factors are (1) assignment of responsibility and (2) accuracy of information. The team must be sure that the person (or people) chosen to collect data understands his or her responsibility and has clear instructions about what, when, and how to collect and what, when, how, and where to record what is collected. We strongly recommend that the team explain why data collection is required. That will give a basic understanding of what the team is trying to accomplish, relieve anxiety, and instill a sense of accountability and ownership in the project.

The information collected must be accurate so that the project team can determine when action is required and can track the progress of the project. Inaccurate data can lull the team into a false sense of security or send members into a frenzy of ghost chasing. So, it is a good idea that a periodic audit of the measurement system and data gathering be conducted by one or more team members. They should be accompanied by representatives from manufacturing engineering and accounting. Verifying the data gives the team a clear picture of the effectiveness of its efforts.

When defining the parameters of the measurement system, the team must also consider the cost of data collection relative to timing. An involved system for collecting, recording, and reporting data on every shift would not be necessary or justifiable if the team only required weekly reporting. On the other hand, labor elements, for example, must be collected (but not necessarily reported) at least on every shift if the performance measurements are productivity, utilizataion, or efficiency. So, a balance must be struck between the risk of not capturing key data and the cost of collecting and reporting information. We recommend (in most projects) that team members review the measurements formally or informally each workday in order to understand the reasons for high and low performances. The project team then will formally review the performance as a group at its weekly meeting.

The team also must consider the cost of accuracy when establishing the system. Accurate information is important, but keeping all things in perspective, the measurement system will be used to indicate the progress of the project, not to balance the general ledger. Therefore the team should keep the system as simple and inexpensive as possible.

The format of data collection and reporting will again depend on the type of data, frequency of collection, and relative cost of collection. Table 3.2 shows a typical example of a computer report displaying efficiency, utilization, and productivity. The team must consider what information it actually needs when designing forms for data collection and reporting.

The performance measurement data collected and reported are only as valuable as the action the team takes after receiving that information. Team activity includes solving problems, implementing changes, and, perhaps, measuring processes differently than before. This activity is focused on achieving the target objective, and the performance measurement system indicates the effect of these activities.

TABLE 3.2 Efficiency, Utilization, and Productivity Report

Week no.	Dept.	(1) Actual hours	(2) Quantity processed	(3) Earned hours	(4) Available hours [(1)+(8)]	(5) Percent efficiency [(3)/(1)]	(6) Percent utilization [(1)/(4)]	(7) Percent productivity [(3)/(4)]	Indirect hours (8) Total	Training	Meetings	Down time	Waiting parts	Medical	Other
1	64122	854.50	153347	1391.49	913.70	162.84	93.52	152.29	59.20	2.00	1.70	0.00	0.00	0.00	55.50
2	64122	1258.00	79326	921.50	1316.50	73.25	95.56	70.00	58.50	3.20	7.60	0.00	4.80	0.00	42.90
3	64122	1211.60	160031	1562.86	1306.00	128.99	92.77	119.67	94.40	20.00	4.90	3.40	0.00	0.00	66.10
4	64122	1064.90	110948	1132.24	1139.60	106.32	93.45	99.35	74.70	7.00	0.00	5.70	0.00	4.00	58.00
Monthly totals		4389.00	503652	5008.09	4675.80	114.11	93.87	107.11	286.80	32.20	14.20	9.10	4.80	4.00	222.50
1	64126	396.00	337	502.83	409.20	126.98	96.77	122.88	13.20	0.00	0.00	0.00	13.20	0.00	0.00
2	64126	445.80	282	503.33	466.90	112.90	95.48	107.80	21.10	0.00	2.20	6.00	7.90	0.00	5.00
3	64126	434.30	271	469.42	469.50	108.09	92.50	99.98	35.20	0.00	1.80	2.10	22.30	0.00	9.00
4	64126	447.90	401	572.33	464.00	127.78	96.53	123.35	16.10	0.00	0.00	2.50	10.60	0.00	3.00
Monthly totals		1724.00	1291	2047.91	1809.60	118.79	95.27	113.17	85.60	0.00	4.00	10.60	54.00	0.00	17.00
1	64134	383.70	298	234.00	429.00	60.99	89.44	54.55	45.30	0.00	10.70	0.40	2.00	0.00	32.20
2	64134	474.30	761	628.50	522.50	132.51	90.78	120.29	48.20	0.00	13.80	0.10	6.10	0.00	28.20
3	64134	515.10	586	478.67	580.00	92.93	80.81	82.53	64.90	0.00	3.50	2.60	7.70	0.00	51.10
4	64134	573.50	650	528.58	623.90	92.17	91.92	84.72	50.40	1.50	0.00	4.00	7.60	0.00	37.30
Monthly totals		1946.60	2295	1869.75	2155.40	96.05	90.31	86.75	208.80	1.50	28.00	7.10	23.40	0.00	148.80
Weekly Plant Composite															
1	All	1634.20	153982	2128.32	1751.90	130.24	93.28	121.49	117.70	2.00	12.40	0.40	15.20	0.00	87.70
2	All	2178.10	80369	2053.33	2305.90	94.27	94.46	89.05	127.80	3.20	23.60	6.10	18.80	0.00	76.10
3	All	2161.00	160888	2510.95	2355.50	116.19	91.74	106.60	194.50	20.00	10.20	8.10	30.00	0.00	126.20
4	All	2086.30	111999	2233.15	2227.50	107.04	93.66	100.25	141.20	8.50	0.00	12.20	18.20	4.00	98.30
Monthly totals		8059.60	507238	8925.75	8640.80	110.75	93.27	103.30	581.20	33.70	46.20	26.80	82.20	4.00	388.30

Timely analysis of the data is a critical factor in the team's decision-making process and project planning. A favorable trend in performance tells the team that its activities are working in the right direction and it can continue with the plan. An unfavorable trend warns the team that action is required. That action includes investigating and understanding the low performance, and the development of a recovery plan. The recovery plan may be a miniproject to determine the cause and the specific action required to bring performance back on track. The recovery plan also assigns responsibilities for actions and target completion deadlines.

Report the Performance

In addition to the performance measurement reports that the team receives for evaluation on a daily or weekly basis, performance will also be reported as part of the project team's weekly report to the steering committee. The format of that information may be as simple as:

Percent defective		
Last week or past month	This week	Objective
10%	9%	2%

In addition to reporting the raw data, the team should prepare a performance graph and include it with the weekly report. The performance graph gives a clear visual picture of the progress of the project and supplements the data. An example is shown in Fig. 3.1, which displays

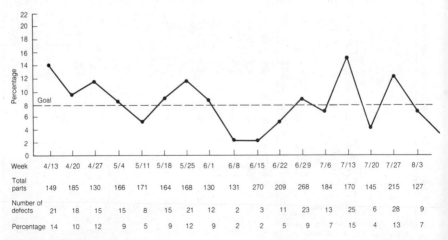

Week	4/13	4/20	4/27	5/4	5/11	5/18	5/25	6/1	6/8	6/15	6/22	6/29	7/6	7/13	7/20	7/27	8/3
Total parts	149	185	130	166	171	164	168	130	131	270	209	268	184	170	145	215	127
Number of defects	21	18	15	15	8	15	21	12	2	3	11	23	13	25	6	28	9
Percentage	14	10	12	9	5	9	12	9	2	2	5	9	7	15	4	13	7

Figure 3.1 Performance graph.

percent defective along with some relative key data. The vertical axis is a scale of the performance measurement, and the horizontal axis is a scale of time in days, weeks, or months. The goal or target of the objective is shown on the graph as a dashed line. Indicating only the goal level on the graph is really not enough. The objective should be time bounded; for example, it should say reduce percent defective from 10 to 2% in four months. The graph should show the project deadline as well.

Between today and the objective target date, intermediate milestones should be established, as shown in Fig. 3.2. These benchmarks, or subtargets, further help the team and others to determine how the project is progressing. They warn when the project is off target and indicate when extra action is required if progress is not meeting expectations. If performance is off target or lower than expected, then a recovery plan should be developed and included as a part of the performance report in the project team's weekly report.

SUMMARY

Completing the foregoing steps is the ultimate responsibility of the team leader working with and directing the activities of the team members. Establishing the measurement criteria, developing the measurement system, deciding on the data collection parameters, monitoring and analyzing reports, and developing recovery plans are all team activities. However, establishing and assigning responsibilities for implementing the system, collecting data, and incremental activities within those steps is the job of the team leader. The leader also reports project performance to the steering committee. The team leader must be the

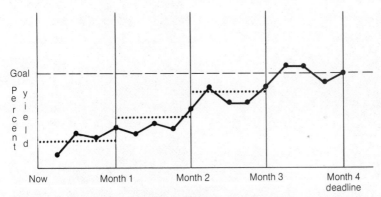

Figure 3.2 Performance graph. Dotted lines represent intermediate benchmark goals between the present time and the target completion date.

moving force to bring the members together on required decisions and to focus their activities so that this major step in the PQI process can be closed.

The closure point occurs when the performance measurement criteria are established, elements of the measurement system are assigned and implemented, and reports to the team are issued. The team then moves to step 4, problem analysis and solution.

4

Problem Analysis and Solution*

At this stage the team has identified and justified its project with a clear objective and plan of attack and is ready to move from the administrative phase (steps 1–3) into the implementation phase of the process. This chapter deals with step 4, problem analysis and solution, which is addressed early in the process because it is an iterative step. This means the team will probably repeat part or all of this step throughout the remaining steps as other problems are identified. Implementation of SPC is most effective when problems are resolved as soon as they are identified, since the emphasis of SPC should be on prevention instead of detection.

In the preceding step, performance measurements were established so that progress of the project could be assessed. Data are now being collected and should be plotted on a chart or graph. The team now has a better idea of the magnitude of the problem requiring resolution by observing the variance from the current level of performance to the stated objective. This chapter presents some proven techniques for problem analysis, including events logs, diagnostic process audits, cause-and-effect diagrams, cause analysis, and design of experiments.

It sometimes happens that the team is implementing projects where step 4 does not appear to be immediately needed. This usually occurs when a process seems to be very efficient with high-quality output. We strongly recommend that the team complete step 4 anyway, because if problems are not already apparent they will usually surface after

---

*Ignacio Munoz participated in preparing this chapter.

conducting inspection capability and process capability studies. The team will then be armed with problem-solving tools and be ready to use them without any delays.

An example is a company beginning to implement SPC on its printed-circuit-board assembly line. The observed quality at final inspection was better than 99%, and the team thought step 4 would not be needed. It conducted an inspection capability study, which indicated that the capability in one area was unacceptable: The inspectors tended to allow some bad product to go through while rejecting good product. The reason for good quality at final inspection was not the result of a good process, but because the product was being prescreened through a "touch-up" operation during the process. Identification of this situation led to a cause-and-effect analysis and eventual solution to the problem. The touch-up operation as it existed was eliminated and is now only performed by exception.

The techniques described in this chapter are not new but are highly recommended for their practicality and effectiveness for systematically addressing each step of the traditional problem-solving approach:

1. State and define the problem
2. Work on the problem and get the facts
3. Restate the problem in light of the new facts
4. Analyze the information and form conclusions
5. Carry out the conclusion and take action
6. Follow-up

Since each situation is unique in character and complexity, so too are the techniques presented. It is important to apply the proper technique to a problem. Let us define a problem as "a deviation from a given standard or desired level of performance for which the cause is unknown and a resolution is required." So before any technique is applied, each key element of the definition must be present.

Events Log

One of the first assignments should be to implement an events log on the process being addressed. The log, similar to a diary, is usually located at or near a critical workstation where control charts are posted. Its purpose is to maintain a chronological history of anything new, different, or changed in or around the process. This is a valuable tool for preventing and solving problems because *any* variation in the process that causes an out-of-control condition is a direct result of something new, different, or changed. Thus the probability is very high that with a properly maintained events log the cause of an out-of-control condition will already have been identified and recorded!

Maintaining the events log is good discipline for those responsible for the process and helps them become more aware of their work environment and to look for changes in their process. They should record the results, whether favorable or unfavorable, of any special tests or studies. That discipline makes problem prevention possible and turns a "fire fighter" into a proactive contributor.

Events can be any changes in people, materials, environment, measurements, methods, machines, or suppliers. Key events, however, will differ from process to process. For example, environment will usually be more critical to a chemical process than to a manufacturing assembly operation. So when establishing and introducing the events log, the team must identify and communicate those parameters deemed critical to the process to people responsible for maintaining the log. Then the people in the process will have a good mental framework where particular awareness is needed.

The events log is easy to implement and maintain. Anyone directly or indirectly associated with or involved in the process can make entries. The format can be as simple as Fig. 4.1 or as involved as Fig. 4.2. The important point is that whatever form it is in, the log must be practical for those making the entries or resistance to using the log will be encountered. Figure 4.1 is recommended as a starter. If it results in "quality" entries, then continue using it. If the entries are meaningless, then a structured format such as Fig. 4.2 might be more appropriate. This structure can also be the vehicle to communicate those elements that are considered important to record.

Diagnostic Process Audits

The second easiest technique to use is the diagnostic process audit, which can be conducted by one person. The problem might even be solved then and there, but even if it is not solved, important information for the cause-and-effect diagram will have been obtained.

Traditionally process audits have been used to verify that what is supposed to be in place is in place, and that people are complying to the process. However, a process audit—usually defined as a thorough, comprehensive survey of every aspect of the process—can be a powerful problem-solving tool when we change its primary focus from *verification* to *diagnosis*. To diagnose is to carefully examine and analyze the facts in an attempt to understand or explain something. The verification function is not eliminated but augmented by asking, what is contributing to a known undesirable condition? Process audits analyze a production or inspection process and provide assurance that the

Events Log

Date	Time	Comments	Date	Time	Comments

Figure 4.1 Events log.

Systems Daily Events Log

Operator changes*   Inspector changes*   Product line: _____
_____   _____   Station: _____
_____   _____   Date: _____
_____   _____   Shift: _____
_____   _____   Supervisor's initials: _____

Changes   Explanation
_____
Process
Material
Tooling
DCO† cut-in
Other
Machine setup
Process
Control chart

Configuration mix (nonstandard products)

Part number   Quantity   Total quantity produced: _____
_____   _____
_____   _____   Yield: _____
_____   _____

Material shortages

           New shortages   Shortages filled

Part number   Part number
_____   _____
_____   _____
_____   _____
_____   _____
                                                  _____

* New operator or inspector, change in operator or inspector.   † Drawing-change order.

Figure 4.2 Systems daily events log.

59

process documentation, tools, and material support are current and feasible for a continuous process that produces acceptable product.

The following outlined procedure will help the team to plan and conduct a diagnostic process audit and to coordinate corrective and preventive action. As the team conducts the audit, it must continuously ask, What about this element could be done differently to prevent the problem in question?

1. Plan the audit.
    a. Define the problem clearly and specifically, in the form of a variance from a standard or desired state.
    b. Identify the process or portion of the process where the variance is observed or originating.
    c. Collect the latest revision of all documents used to establish and maintain the subject process, such as assembly instructions, workmanship standards, inspection instructions, test instructions, fabrication methods, product specifications, calibration procedures, tooling drawings, station layout, and training records.
    d. Select the individual(s) and station(s) to be audited. If more than one operator is assigned per station, select the operator who most closely represents the average skill level.
    e. Select the audit team. As a minimum the audit team must be composed of the production supervisor, process engineer, quality engineer, and quality engineering supervisor. If necessary the production lead person, production operator, inspection lead person, inspector, or test engineer may be included.
2. Conduct the audit.
    a. Before conducting the physical audit, verify and understand the inspection and assembly methods and verify that all documents are current and complete.
    b. Inform the responsible line supervisor that an audit will be performed and obtain the required interface support. Unless special circumstances warrant it, no advance notice is required.
    c. Introduce the auditor(s) to the operator or inspector and explain the purpose of the audit to him or her.
    d. Conduct the audit using checklists found in Chap. 12 (Figs. 12.1–12.3). Record the audit findings. Indicate if the element is acceptable or unacceptable according to the current requirements, and if it, regardless of its status, could be further improved to prevent the problem in question. The following audit sequence is recommended:
        (1) Review documentation at the station being audited for availability, currentness, and completeness.

    (2) Review tools and gages for conformance to methods and calibration.

    (3) Review station layout for conformance to plans.

    (4) Review material handling in, around, and out of the station.

    (5) Review the human factors.

    (6) Review the machine setups.

    (7) Audit the production and inspection processes.

3. Establish the corrective and preventive action.

    a. Review the resulting audit deficiencies and opportunities with the audit team. Wherever possible, take immediate corrective action to resolve deficiencies.

    b. Develop preventive actions for the opportunities identified.

    c. Develop a plan for implementing preventive actions that includes specifics about what will be done, who will do it, and when it will be done.

    d. Obtain commitment from responsible individuals.

    e. Follow-up, follow-up, follow-up through the entire audit process.

4. Report to management using the following items as a guideline for the main sections. A well-written, concise report of an important audit will result in positive and timely action on the recommendations.

    a. State the purpose of the audit.

    b. Briefly describe how, where, why the audit was carried out.

    c. State findings and conclusions as a result of the audit.

    d. Recommend a corrective and preventive action plan.

Cause-and-Effect Diagrams

The cause-and-effect diagram, better known as the Ishikawa diagram, relates an observed effect with its possible causes. When completed the diagram resembles a fishbone and is often referred to as a *fishbone diagram.* It requires minimum training to apply and takes advantage of the problem-solving synergism created by a group of people.

Causes are variables or factors that contribute to the variation or level of the resultant effect. Causes can usually be categorized by people, machine, methods, materials, measurements, or movement. The *effect* is usually a performance characteristic that results from a specific cause and is manifested in a symptom.

Figure 4.3 is an example of a completed cause-and-effect diagram. The *effect* in this example is "part shortages in kits at kit staging." This effect could manifest itself in production schedules not being met. It is important to distinguish an effect and a symptom. Otherwise, personnel will address the wrong problem, and the symptom will be an unresolved problem.

To prepare a cause-and-effect diagram follow this procedure.

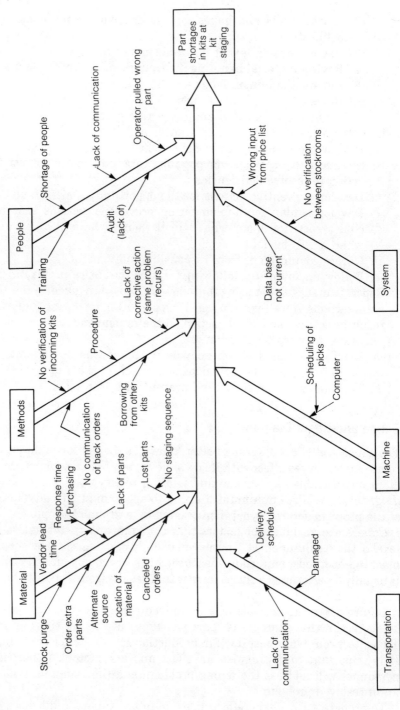

Figure 4.3 Cause-and-effect diagram.

62

1. *Initiate the meeting.*   Invite all personnel affected by the problem who have knowledge and experience about it. Include operators and inspectors as well as managers. For a product quality problem, consider anyone in the organization from product development and design to customer service. The team leader usually conducts the meeting.

2. *Clarify the effect.*   The actual problem must be refined and defined so that a clear statement of the effect is established. This will reduce the influence of unrelated causes. When the problem is too large or obscure, break the problem into several smaller elements. Then construct a cause-and-effect diagram for each element.

Write the problem effect to the right of the backbone, as shown in Fig. 4.4.

The problem or effect can be a quality characteristic such as percentage of defective products, strength, size, or weight. It might be an economic characteristic such as yield, working hours, energy consumption, response time, or production rate, or an environmental characteristic such as pollution, turnover of personnel, or accident frequency.

3. *Generate causes by brainstorming methods.*   Identify the major groups of causes as branches from the main backbone. Suggested major branches are people, materials, methods, machine, measurements, and movement, as in Fig. 4.4. Generate potential causes by asking each attendee to present one cause. Write each cause on the diagram on the appropriate branch. Continue adding subbranches as needed. It may take several rounds to obtain all the causes, so continue the process until two rounds are made where everyone passes. For example, suppose for a given effect that lack of training is identified as a potential cause. This would be shown as in Fig. 4.5.

New causes may arise from new associations of other members' causes. Usually these will support or further clarify the causes listed on the major branch. For the lack-of-training example someone may suggest that people are not following procedures. The cause would be added to the diagram as in Fig. 4.6.

Observe the rules of brainstorming: (1) be courteous; (2) encourage new ideas; (3) make no judgments. When all causes have been presented, encourage discussion for or against any cause to clarify or justify ideas before voting. If someone has strong supporting informa-

Effect

Figure 4.4 Effect backbone of cause-and-effect diagram.

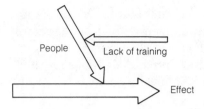

Figure 4.5   Causes are added to cause-and-effect diagram.

tion or opinions that others might not have, let that person share this information. Then make a final check to see that all causes are included in the diagram.

4. *Determine the importance of causes.*   After two clear passes have been made, take a vote on all causes. Use two rounds of voting. In the first round each cause is stated and attendees may vote for as many causes that they feel are critical. The top 10 causes, based on the number of votes, are then selected for the second round of voting. The attendees now vote on only one of the 10 causes; each attendee has only *one* vote in this round. The cause with the largest vote count in the second round is selected as the first priority to address. Other causes with high vote counts should be given priorities and documented for further investigation.

5. *Verify the cause.*   Verify that the cause selected does affect the process characteristic through methods such as design of experiments, data collection, or control charts.

6. *Take corrective action.*   The method for verifying the cause might provide the appropriate corrective action. If not, or if the methods used for verification are not practical under production conditions, then hold another brainstorming session.

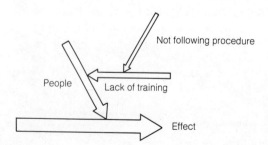

Figure 4.6   Construction of cause-and-effect diagram continues.

Cause Analysis

Cause analysis is a process developed by Alamo Learning Systems, Inc., Walnut Creek, California. It is one section of a training program for process management skills (PMS). The other sections include decision making, plan analysis, and situation review.

The cause-analysis technique uses a structured method of questioning (the process) that taps the relevant information about problems. Brainstorming is not used. The goal of the process is to draw out precise information. *Precise* in this sense means definite, exact, accurate, and specifically stated information. It is a process of comparison and then creating comparative test bases. Its advantage is the high quality of the results generated. Only known facts and relevant information are used to draw out likely causes.

When using cause analysis, the manager should think of the problem as an iceberg—what is seen initially only hints at the entire problem. Through the analysis managers can then determine the actual size and scope of the problem. They can better understand the problem by collecting more data until they can see the whole iceberg. However, they still may be unable to deal with the problem unless they classify the data into a useful format, separating the relevant from the irrelevant. They do not need to collect data on the entire "polar cap" in order to put a particular iceberg into proper focus.

Cause analysis provides the format to help classify data and is a guide for collecting only relevant data in terms of what, where, when, and magnitude.

Because this technique is very structured, it requires more training than a cause-and-effect diagram does. This might be a limiting factor in the selection of a problem-solving method. To learn more about this process, refer to Lorne C. Plunkett and Guy A. Hale, *The Proactive Manager.*

Design of Experiments

Design of experiments is an effective method of problem analysis for improving manufacturing processes and for exploring product and process improvements during the design and development stages.*

The objective of a designed experiment is usually to determine which of the many variables or causes most influence some response or output

---

*The Japanese use design of experiment concepts as part of the "off-line" quality control methods developed by Genichi Taguchi, often referred to as the Taguchi approach. These methods have been very effective in electrical circuit analysis for selecting components.

variable. The designed experiment is the only way of properly evaluating and quantifying the interaction between the variables.

A designed experiment can be described as a box with several knobs, called *factors,* on one side and a meter on the other side, which displays the result or effect of turning the knobs (see Fig. 4.7). Each knob can be moved to one or more positions (on/off, a/b/c, etc.), referred to as the *levels of the factors.* The output meter reading changes as the knobs are changed from position to position. This reading is called the *output* or *response* of the experiment. A typical objective of a designed experiment might be to determine which factor (knob) produces the largest change in the output (meter). The result of changing knob A from position 1 to position 2 may produce the result shown in Fig. 4.7. This change in the response is called the *effect* of factor A.

Measuring the interaction between factors is one of the most powerful results of a designed experiment. No other experimental method can properly evaluate this interaction. Figure 4.8 illustrates the concept with two factors. The top graph illustrates *no* interaction. When factor A is changed, the same change or effect occurs no matter what the level of factor B. The bottom graph illustrates *interaction.* The same effect does not occur at both levels of factor B.

The method of data collection for designed experiments involves randomization techniques, which determine the effects of all factors as if they were changed one at a time and will also evaluate interactions. To perform a design of experiments, follow these steps for a properly designed, conducted, analyzed, and presented experiment: (1) plan the

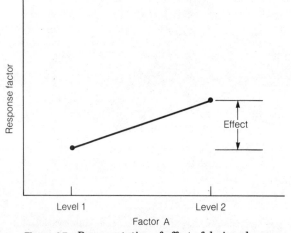

Figure 4.7   Representation of effect of designed experiment.

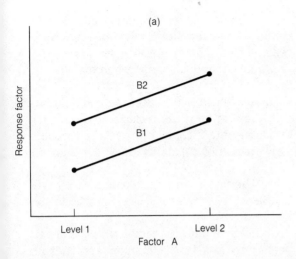

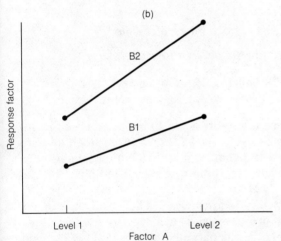

Figure 4.8 Representations of interaction between two factors of designed experiment. (*a*) No interaction. (*b*) Interaction.

experiment, (2) develop the design, (3) conduct the experiment, (4) perform the analysis, and (5) report the results.

Plan the experiment

State the problem or objective. State why the experiment is to be performed. Avoid vagueness, excessive ambition, and extensive generalities. The objective often contains the factors (causes) and response or output (effects) to be studied. For example: Determine the effects and interactions of the speed and feed of a machining operation on tool wear. The factors are speed and feed, and the response is tool wear.

Determine response variable(s) measurement. Select the method for quantifying the response variable. Determine if the response will be variable data or attribute data. Determine the capability of the response measurement by performing an inspection capability study (see Chap. 5).

Choose the factors and levels. The factors are the variables that will be studied in the experiment. Select the levels to be used for each factor.

Develop a milestone plan. A milestone plan for conducting the experiment ensures that it is performed in a timely manner and that all steps are performed completely.

Develop the design

Developing the design consists of two major elements:

1. *Determine the total number of observations as follows:*

Total observations = (Number of combinations) ×
(Number of readings per combination)

The number of combinations is usually equal to the number of factors multiplied by the number of levels for each factor. In experiments where the number of factors is greater than 5, not all combinations need to be run. A fraction may be run according to a structured plan. This is referred to as a *fractional factorial.*

2. *Determine the order of running the experiment.* The experiment is usually run in a random order, which is achieved by the technique of randomization. Randomization is obtained from a table of random numbers or other random-number generators. This is critical in order to prevent other variables from biasing the results or being mixed in with effects and interactions of the factors being studied. Determining the order of running the experiment is important to see if there are any further variables or restrictions on the randomization that need to be considered.

Some experiments restrict the randomization due to practical limitations in an experimental environment. These restrictions can be handled effectively with designed experiment methods. The names of experiments that handle restrictions are randomized blocks, nested designs, or split-plot designs.

Develop the data collection procedure and forms. The random order developed in the previous step is documented since this becomes the road map to follow in collecting the data. Develop the data recording forms so that they coordinate with the random order determined. These forms should also facilitate translating data to a computer for analysis. Decide who will do the actual data recording—the operator, inspector, engineer, or someone else? Knowledge of the method of analysis to be used is helpful in developing useful data recording forms.

Conduct the experiment

Provide an overview of the experiment to all personnel involved along with an explanation of data collection procedures and data recording forms.

Conduct and monitor the experiment. Close monitoring of the actual data collection is required in order to ensure that biases (intentional or unintentional) are not introduced into the experiment.

Record data on appropriate forms. Monitor the data recording very closely at the start of the experiment to ensure accuracy and minimum recording errors.

Initiate an events log. Initiate an events log before running the experiment to record all major changes that occur during the experiment. This will be very helpful if the analysis indicates unusual or unexpected results.

Perform the analysis

Prepare for the analysis. Obtain the data sheets and prepare data for the analysis method. Enter the data into the appropriate computer file if computers are used.

Perform the analysis. The computations are carried out by the analysis method appropriate for the experimental design.

Summarize the analysis. Summarize the results of the analysis for incorporation in the report. All results should be interpreted in terms that are *meaningful* to personnel who will be using the results.

Report the results

Prepare the report using the following items as a guideline for the main sections. A well-written and concise report of an important experiment will result in positive and timely action on the recommendations. It is often helpful to clarify the results by using tables and graphs to present the data.

- Objective: State the reason for the experiment.
- Methodology: Briefly describe how the experiment was performed.
- Findings and conclusions: What was actually found?
- Recommendations: What should be done?
- Resources required: What is required to implement the recommendations?
- Analysis: Give the details of the design and analysis of the data.

SUMMARY

Table 4.1 summarizes guidelines to help the team decide which problem-solving technique is most appropriate, so the team will be most effective and efficient in solving the problems it will encounter throughout the balance of the PQI process.

TABLE 4.1   Problem-solving method application selections

| | Problem-solving method | | | |
	Events log	Cause and effect diagram	Cause analysis	Design of experiments
Typical applications	Implement as part of process control procedure. Expected performance of process or product has experienced a sudden change. Implement at each specific machine or assembly operation. Source of information for what is new, changed, or different in process.	Generates possible causes of repetitive problems. Generates possible CP actions for out-of-control points on control charts. Facilitates breakthroughs to improve levels of productivity and quality.	Expected performance of process or product has experienced a sudden change. Identifies causes of repetitive problems. Time-related problems. Facilitates breakthroughs to improve levels of productivity and quality. Expected performance of process or product has not been met since day 1.	Concerned with many variables or factors effecting a response. Determines which of many factors are significant.

TABLE 4.1 Problem-solving method application selections (*Continued*)

	Problem-solving method			
	Events log	Cause and effect diagram	Cause analysis	Design of experiments
Advantages	Provides immediate and ongoing feedback to identify causes for out-of-control points, process shifts, or trends. Easy to implement and maintain.	Involves operators and inspectors. Uses synergistic resources of the group (PQI team). Minimum of training needed to implement. Ideas or causes generated by brainstorming methods.	Detailed technical knowledge or experience of process or product not required. Uses synergistic resources of the group (PQI team). Efficiently narrows possible causes to one or two. Provides a systematic method for organizing thoughts for a complex problem.	Identifies significant factors or variables. Identifies interaction of variables. Randomization eliminates hidden biases in results. Structured approach to designing and running experiment.
Disadvantages	Requires ongoing effort to maintain. Easy to omit events that may not appear important but are.	Priority of investigating causes determined by experience of group. Very little data and facts are used to generate causes. Not efficient for complex problems. Requires technical knowledge and experience with the product or process.	Initial use of method may be time-consuming. Workshop attendance required for ongoing use.	Requires knowledge of experimental design methods to set up and analyze. Requires discipline in running experiment to prescribed order.
Skill level	Low	Medium	Medium	High
Training amount	Low	Low	High	High
Ease of implementation	Easy	Medium	Medium to complex	Complex

TABLE 4.1   Problem-solving method application selections (*Continued*)

	Problem-solving method			
	Events log	Cause and effect diagram	Cause analysis	Design of experiments
Size of group involved in solving problem		Medium to large	Medium	Small
Usefulness of results	Immediate feedback. Operators, inspectors, supervisors make entries.	Generates numerous ideas. Includes operators and inspectors. Priorities determined by vote.	Good at identifying most likely causes. Process complex but very helpful for organizing and focusing thought process.	Best used to test causes. Very efficient at determining critical factors from among many possibilities. Identifies interaction effects among causes.

5

Inspection Capability*

The project team has now identified more specifically the problem area, and it may have used some of the problem-solving techniques described in the last chapter. If the team decides to do further analysis or gather data about the process, then before implementing SPC, it should apply the powerful and critical technique called inspection capability (IC), step 5 of the PQI process.

It is often taken for granted that inspection results are true values with no error—it is simply assumed that measurements taken in a manufacturing operation are correct. However, even inspection methods are subject to variation, whether the results are derived from a basic mechanical measuring device, complex electronic gear, or a simple go/no-go gage. Even if this fact is known, an evaluation of the consequences is seldom made. The possibility of fluctuating results is usually neglected.

The output-oriented production person may take advantage of the situation by sending the rejected part back for retest or reinspection. The part may pass the second time, or the third time, or the fourth. In such a situation, however, others in manufacturing will lose faith in SPC and it will never achieve its savings potential.

Inspection capability is a method for evaluating and quantifying an existing inspection system. The key feature of this method is to ensure that accurate data are obtained for ongoing SPC. Inspection capability, then, can be considered the "missing link" in the successful implementation of SPC. This chapter defines IC and discusses methods for determining IC and gathering data for variable (measurement) and attribute

---

*Wendell Paulson participated in preparing this chapter.

(visual inspection) data; analyzing, evaluating, and reporting the results of the IC study; and corrective action; and gives examples of IC studies and checklists.

Inspection Capability Study

Inspection capability studies determine if an inspection method or piece of equipment produces acceptable, marginal, or unacceptable results. IC studies are to

- Evaluate new measuring equipment or inspection methods
- Compare one or more of the same type of measuring equipment
- Compare measuring equipment before and after repair or adjustment
- Compare inspection techniques between suppliers and between the suppliers' final inspection and the customer's receiving inspection

The major steps of an IC study are as follows:

1. Describe the study by specifying the inspection method, type of data, and the purpose of the study; develop a plan.
2. Prepare the data collection method for the appropriate type of data (variable or attribute).
3. Collect and record the data on the appropriate form.
4. Follow the appropriate data computation procedure.
5. Evaluate the results and determine if the study is acceptable, marginal, or unacceptable, using the criteria provided.
6. Establish the required corrective action and follow-up for marginal or unacceptable studies.
7. Report the results.
8. Repeat the study after any corrective action is complete.

IC studies measure and quantify the repeatability and reproducibility of the measurement and inspection method.

Repeatability

Repeatability is the variation resulting from the inability of the measuring instrument to obtain the same result repeatedly, due to the numerous little things that make up the measuring system (friction, springs, etc.) and the inability of the checker to operate and read the instrument exactly the same way every time. This situation should more properly be called *lack of repeatability,* since no variation would occur if the measuring instrument were repeatable.

Repeatability may be determined by measuring the same part several times. The resulting distribution of the measurements is shown in Fig. 5.1. The spread, or 6σ, of this distribution should be small when compared to the total tolerance [upper specification limit (USL) minus lower specification limit (LSL)].

For attribute data repeatability is defined to be the variation in classifying parts as conforming or nonconforming when one person inspects the same part several times using the same inspection method, criteria, or equipment.

Reproducibility

Reproducibility is the variation among the people doing the measurements or inspection using the same methods or equipment. It is more properly called *lack of reproducibility.* The variation among identical measuring instruments used by the same person is another source of lack of reproducibility.

Reproducibility may be determined by having another person measure the same parts with the same measuring instrument. The distribution of the results of the second person is shown in Fig. 5.2 as distribution B. Distribution A in Fig. 5.2 is the results of the first person. The difference between the averages of the readings in distributions A and B is the measure of reproducibility.

Reproducibility for attribute data is defined as the variation among people inspecting the same parts using the same inspection method, criteria, or equipment.

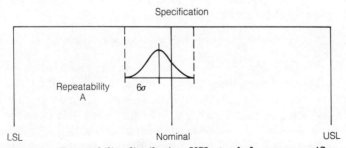

Figure 5.1 Repeatability distribution. USL stands for upper specification limit, LSL for lower specification limit.

Specification

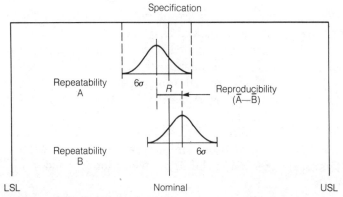

Figure 5.2   Reproducibility.

Inspection Capability

Repeatability and reproducibility are quantified and combined to determine the IC. For variable data the percentage of the total tolerance consumed by the capability (PTCC) is calculated. For attribute data the capability cannot be expressed as a percentage of a tolerance. The emphasis for attribute data is on how effective a person is at detecting conforming or nonconforming parts and how biased a person is toward rejecting conforming parts or accepting nonconforming parts.

This chapter describes methods for determining IC for variable and attribute data. The end result of the study is to determine if the measurement and inspection method is acceptable, marginal, or unacceptable according to given criteria. An acceptable IC study is required before a process capability study is performed (refer to Chap. 6).

Inspection Capability Study for Variable Data

This section contains information on collecting, analyzing, and evaluating IC studies involving variable data. When a part is measured, each reading obtained on a single piece consists of the true value, a constant error, and the repeatability error:

Reading = True value + constant error + repeatability error

The true value of a part does not change when repeat measurements are made on it. The deviation from the true value occurs because the measuring instrument is off calibration; it is the same for all readings and is thus called the constant error. The IC study described here for variable data is concerned only with repeatability error.

The effect of repeatability and reproducibility on the readings is shown in Fig. 5.3. The effect is to enlarge the tolerance. The vertical

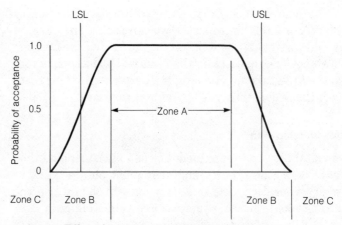

Figure 5.3   Effect of inspection capability on tolerance.

axis is the probability of acceptance, and the horizontal axis is the tolerance. The curve shows that the probability of accepting a part increases from 0 to 1.0 in zone B, remains constant in zone A, and decreases from 1.0 to 0 in zone B. All parts will be accepted in zone A, and rejected in zone C. In zone B some good parts will be rejected, and some bad parts will be accepted.

The curve in Fig. 5.3 is for a gage of repeatability equal to 40% of the tolerance. The width of zone B is equal to the repeatability of 40% or two-fifths of the tolerance. The repeatability causes the specification to be "stretched" above the USL and below the LSL by half the width of zone B. The net result is an increase in the specification width by an amount equal to the total width of zone B, which is two-fifths of the tolerance. Thus the specification width is increased by an amount equal to the percentage of tolerance consumed by the repeatability of the measuring instrument. Regardless of the type of equipment or the part to be measured, this curve always exists. If the repeatability of the measuring instrument is 10% instead of 40%, the specification is increased by 10%.

As the tolerance grows wider the gray area becomes narrower as a percentage of tolerance, and vice versa. In some cases the gray zone may be larger than the entire tolerance (repeatability is greater than 100% of the tolerance)—it might then be better to stop measuring and roll dice to determine if the part should be accepted!

When the repeatability percentage of tolerance is too large (greater than, say, 20%), the repeatability must be reduced by working on the instrument or buying a new one. Sometimes it cannot be reduced even after much effort. For example, suppose a tolerance less than 0.001 is required and the measurements are performed on a coordinate measuring machine to the nearest 0.00005 in. An acceptable repeatability value is 10% of 0.001 or 0.001. In this case we can reduce the effect of repeatability by making repeat readings on the part using the average of the values obtained. The repeatability is reduced by the square root of the number of readings taken. For example, the average of four readings has only half the repeatability of individual readings.

Data collection for variable data

To determine repeatability and reproducibility of a measuring method involving variable data, the quality engineer must obtain parts or samples from every appraiser. The quality engineer should use the following guidelines when selecting samples and collecting data.

1. Randomly select parts from production. The parts may or may not be within specifications because the actual size has no effect on repeatability or reproducibility. However, it is best to select parts which represent the total range of the dimensions. Label each part with a number or code to maintain a unique identity and facilitate data collection. The minimum number of samples and repeat measurements required are indicated in Table 5.1.

2. Review the inspection method or instruction and verify that it is current and correct.

3. Review the inspection method with the appraisers. Explain to them the purpose of the study, the method of data collection, and the role of the appraisers.

4. Measure each part once in a random order and record the readings on a data sheet.

TABLE 5.1 Sample Sizes for Inspection Capability Studies Involving Variable Data

Number of appraisers	Number of gages	Minimum number of parts	Minimum number of measurements per part
1	1	10	5
1	2	15	3
2	1		
2	2	10	2
1 or 2	3 or more		
3 or more	1 or 2		
3 or more	3 or more		

5. Measure each part again in a random order and record the readings on another data sheet. It is important to keep the readings separate so that the appraisers are not biased by the previous readings.

6. Continue taking measurements on each part, one at a time, until the desired number of readings per part are obtained. Record each set of readings on separate data sheets.

Data analysis for variable data

The following example illustrates analysis of data from an IC study with variable data.

Example. Obtain the IC of a special probe and validator that measures the tip location in the x and y directions of a matrix printer hammerspring. Only one gage is available, and one appraiser is used. The specification is 0.989 ± 0.003 (0.006 total tolerance).

Only the data relating to the x direction will be illustrated. Since only one gage and one appraiser are used, we select 10 samples and obtain five measurements per sample according to Table 5.1. The measurements are shown in Table 5.2 to the nearest 0.00005 in (the gage increment).

We now compute the range of the repeat readings for each part and record them on the variable data worksheet in Fig. 5.4 in the row identified as the range R. We now compute the average range $(\bar{R})$ across all parts and record it on the data recording sheet in the space identified:

$$\bar{R} = (0.0001 + 0.0001 + \cdots + 0.0001)/10$$
$$= 0.0015/10 = 0.00015$$

If more than one person or gage is used, we compute the overall average range by the formula

$$\bar{R} = (\bar{R}_1 + \bar{R}_2 + \cdots + \bar{R}_K)/K$$

TABLE 5.2 Data for Variable Data Analysis Example

		Sample									
	Trial	1	2	3	4	5	6	7	8	9	10
	1	0.9894	0.9895	0.9892	0.9892	0.9894	0.9904	0.9897	0.9900	0.9887	0.9895
	2	0.9894	0.9895	0.9892	0.9890	0.9892	0.9902	0.9898	0.9898	0.9887	0.9895
$\Sigma X =$	3	0.9895	0.9895	0.9893	0.9892	0.9892	0.9903	0.9898	0.9900	0.9888	0.9895
$\bar{X} =$	4	0.9894	0.9896	0.9892	0.9891	0.9891	0.9903	0.9898	0.9900	0.9888	0.9894
$\Sigma R = 0.0015$	5	0.9894	0.9896	0.9892	0.9891	0.9893	0.9902	0.9897	0.9900	0.9887	0.9895
$\bar{R} = 0.00015$	R	0.0001	0.0001	0.0001	0.0002	0.0003	0.0002	0.0001	0.0002	0.0001	0.0001

Variable Data Worksheet

Part number _____ Date _____

Dimension or characteristic _____

Specification or tolerance _____

1. Range evaluation

	Original	Revised	Upper control limit range (UCL$_R$)

$\bar{R}_1 =$_____   _____ $n =$_____ $D_4 =$_____

$\bar{R}_2 =$_____   _____ $UCL_R = D_4\bar{R} =$_____

$\bar{R}_3 =$_____   _____   No. points above $UCL_R =$_____

$\Sigma\bar{R} =$_____   _____   No. points discarded = _____

$\bar{R} =$_____   _____

2. Repeatability evaluation

$SDR = (1/d_2)\bar{R}$ $n =$_____ $1/d_2 =$_____

$SDR =$ _____

Repeatability $= 6 \times SDR =$ _____

$PTCR = [(6 \times SDR)/(\text{Total tol.})] \times 100\% =$ _____

3. Reproducibility evaluation (Appraisers or Gages)

$R_M = \bar{X}_L - \bar{X}_S$ $\bar{X}_L =$_____ $\bar{X}_S =$_____

$R_M =$_____

$SDM = DR_M$ $K =$_____ $D =$_____

$SDM =$ _____

Reproducibility $= 6 \times SDM =$ _____

$PTCM = [(6 \times SDM)/(\text{Total tol.})] \times 100\% =$ _____

4. Inspection capability evaluation

$SDC = \sqrt{(SDR)^2 + (SDM)^2}$

$SDC =$ _____

$PTCC = [(6 \times SDC)/(\text{Total tol.})] \times 100\% =$ _____

Figure 5.4 Variable data worksheet.

where K = number of combinations of persons and gages, and $\bar{R}_1, \bar{R}_2, \ldots, \bar{R}_K$ = average range of each person and gage combination.

The following items from the variable data worksheets in Figs. 5.4 and 5.5 are calculated.

Range evaluation. Compute the upper control limit for the range (UCL_R):

$$\text{UCL}_R = D_4 \bar{R}$$

where D_4 is a factor in Table 5.3 with n = number of repeat readings on each part. The D_4 factor is the same factor used in control charts for the range. In the example, $n = 5$ and $D_4 = 2.114$, and

$$\text{UCL}_R = (2.114)(0.00015) = 0.000317$$

If any range exceeds the UCL_R, do the following:

1. Remeasure the part to determine if the out-of-control range was due to a recording error or a measurement error.

2. If a data recording error is suspected, remove the affected data from the computations and recalculate the average range and UCL_R. If more than one data recording error is found, repeat the study.

3. If there is more than one range exceeding the UCL_R due to a measurement error, the method must be revised. No further computations need be done, and the study should be repeated after the method is revised.

4. If only one range exceeds the UCL_R due to a measurement method error, remove the affected data on that part from the computations and recompute the average range and UCL_R.

In the example, no range exceeds the UCL_R.

Repeatability evaluation. We compute the repeatability, as shown in section 2 on the worksheet, by computing the standard deviation of repeatability (SDR) and multiplying that value by 6:

$$\text{SDR} = (1/d_2)\bar{R}$$

where $1/d_2$ is another control chart factor in Table 5.3. In the example, $1/d_2 = 0.429$ and

$$\text{SDR} = (0.429)(0.00015) = 0.00006435$$

Variable Data Worksheet

Part number _____ Date _____

Dimension or characteristic _____

Specification or tolerance _____ 0.989 ± 0.003 (0.006 total tolerance) _____

1. Range evaluation

    Original   Revised   Upper control limit range (UCL$_R$)

$\bar{R}_1$ = _0.00015_   _____ n = __5__ D_4 = _2.114_

$\bar{R}_2$ = _____   _____   UCL$_R$ = $D_4\bar{R}$ = _0.000317_

$\bar{R}_3$ = _____   _____   No. points above UCL$_R$ = __0__

$\Sigma\bar{R}$ = _____   _____   No. points discarded = __0__

$\bar{R}$ = _____   _____

2. Repeatability evaluation

    SDR = $(1/d_2)\bar{R}$ n = __5__ $1/d_2$ = _0.429_

    SDR = _____0.00006435_____

    Repeatability = 6 x SDR = _____0.000386_____

    PTCR = [(6 x SDR) / (Total tol.)] x 100% = _6.43%_____

3. Reproducibility evaluation (Appraisers or Gages)

    R_M = $\bar{X}_L - \bar{X}_S$ $\bar{X}_L$ = _____ $\bar{X}_S$ = _____

    R_M = _____

    SDM = DR_M K = _____ D = _____

    SDM = _____

    Reproducibility = 6 x SDM = _____

    PTCM = [(6 x SDM) / (Total tol.)] x 100% = _____

4. Inspection capability evaluation

    SDC = $\sqrt{(\text{SDR})^2 + (\text{SDM})^2}$

    SDC = _Same as SDR above_

    PTCC = [(6 x SDC) / (Total tol.)] x 100% = _Same as PTCR above_

Figure 5.5 Example of variable data worksheet for inspection capability study.

**TABLE 5.3 Repeatability Factors
for Inspection Capability Studies
involving Variable Data**

n	$1/d_2$	D_4
2	0.885	3.268
3	0.592	2.574
4	0.485	2.282
5	0.429	2.114

The percent tolerance consumed by repeatability (PTCR) is

$$PTCR = \frac{6 \times SDR}{Total\ tolerance} \times 100$$

In the example:

$$PTCR = \frac{6 \times 0.00006435}{0.006} \times 100$$

$$= \frac{0.000386}{0.006} \times 100 = 6.43\%$$

Reproducibility evaluation. If more than one appraiser or gage is
involved in the study, the reproducibility must be calculated. The following computations are carried out to obtain the average of all readings
for each appraiser or gage. If three gages and two appraisers are used,
the computation is carried out for both the gages and the appraisers.

Find the largest ($\overline{X}_L$) and smallest ($\overline{X}_S$) averages. Compute the difference of these two averages or means:

$$R_M = \overline{X}_L - \overline{X}_S$$

Compute the standard deviation of reproducibility:

$$SDM = DR_M$$

where D = factor in Table 5.4 with K = number of appraisers or gages.

**TABLE 5.4 Reproducibility Factors
for Inspection Capability Studies
involving Variable Data**

K	D
2	0.709
3	0.524
4	0.446
5	0.403

Compute the percent tolerance consumed by reproducibility (PTCM):

$$\text{PTCM} = \frac{6 \times \text{SDM}}{\text{Total tolerance}} \times 100$$

In the example there is only one gage and one appraiser, so the reproducibility cannot be calculated.

IC evaluation. The percent tolerance consumed by IC is

$$\text{PTCC} = \frac{6 \times \text{SDC}}{\text{Total tolerance}} \times 100$$

where

$$\text{SDC} = \sqrt{(\text{SDR})^2 + (\text{SDM})^2}$$

Note: If appraisers and gages are both included in the study, the variance of the reproducibility must be computed for both appraisers and gages and then added to find the overall IC.

In the example, the IC is the same as the repeatability computed earlier.

Data evaluation for variable data

Use the following criteria for PTCC to evaluate the results of the study to determine if the measurement method is acceptable, marginal, or unacceptable.

PTCC value	Study result
10% or less	Acceptable
Between 10 and 25%	Marginal
Greater than 25%	Unacceptable

If the measurement method is unacceptable or marginal, corrective action is required. The study should be repeated when corrective action is completed.

Variable-data examples

Example 1. An IC study is performed using one appraiser and three gages. The total tolerance is 0.002 in, and the measurements were recorded to the nearest 0.0001 in.

With one appraiser and three gages, 10 samples were selected and two measurements per sample were obtained according to Table 5.1. The average range and the average for each gage are as follows:

Gage	$\bar{R}$	$\bar{X}$
A	0.000053	0.00038
B	0.000052	0.00035
C	0.000054	0.00036

The computations are shown on the worksheet in Fig. 5.6. The range evaluation is

$$\text{UCL}_R = D_4\bar{R} = (3.268)(0.000053) = 0.0001732$$

where $D_4 = 3.268$ with $n = 2$ readings per part. Suppose all ranges are less than the UCL_R.
The repeatability evaluation is

$$\text{SDR} = (1/d_2)\bar{R} \quad (0.885)(0.000053) = 0.000047$$

where $1/d_2 = 0.885$ from Table 5.3 for $n = 2$.
The percent tolerance consumed by repeatability is

$$\text{PTCR} = \frac{6 \times 0.000047}{0.002} \times 100 = 14.1\%$$

For the reproducibility evaluation, first compute the standard deviation for reproducibility. We must find the largest and smallest averages of the three gages: $\bar{X}_L = 0.00038$ for gage A; $\bar{X}_S = 0.00035$ for gage B. The range of the three gages is

$$R_M = X_L - \bar{X}_S = 0.00038 - 0.00035 = 0.00003$$

The standard deviation of the gages is

$$\text{SDM} = (0.524)(0.00003) = 0.000016$$

where $D = 0.524$ from Table 5.3 with $K = 3$ gages.
The reproducibility of the gages is

$$\text{Reproducibility} = 6 \times \text{SDM} = 6 \times 0.000016 = 0.000096$$

The percent tolerance of the gages is

$$\text{PTCM} = \frac{\text{Reproducibility}}{\text{Total tolerance}} \times 100$$

$$= \frac{0.000096}{0.002} \times 100 = 4.8\%$$

Variable Data Worksheet

Part number _____ Date _____

Dimension or characteristic _____

Specification or tolerance _____ 0.002 total tolerance _____

1. Range evaluation

	Original	Revised	Upper control limit range (UCL$_R$)

$\bar{R}_1$ = 0.000053 _____ n = __2__ D_4 = 3.268

$\bar{R}_2$ = 0.000052 _____   UCL$_R$ = $D_4\bar{R}$ = 0.0001732

$\bar{R}_3$ = 0.000054 _____   No. points above UCL$_R$ = 0

$\Sigma\bar{R}$ = 0.000159 _____   No. points discarded = 0

$\bar{R}$ = 0.000053 _____

2. Repeatability evaluation

$SDR = (1/d_2)\bar{R}$ n = __2__ $1/d_2$ = 0.885

SDR = 0.000047

Repeatability = 6 x SDR = 0.000282

PTCR = [(6 x SDR) / (Total tol.)] x 100% = 14.1%

3. Reproducibility evaluation (Appraisers or Gages)

$R_M = \bar{X}_L - \bar{X}_S$ $\bar{X}_L$ = 0.00038 $\bar{X}_S$ = 0.00035

R_M = 0.00003

$SDM = DR_M$ K = 3 D = 0.524

SDM = 0.000016

Reproducibility = 6 x SDM = 0.000096

PTCM = [(6 x SDM) / (Total tol.)] x 100% = 4.8%

4. Inspection capability evaluation

$SDC = \sqrt{(SDR)^2 + (SDM)^2}$

SDC = 0.0000496

PTCC = [(6 x SDC) / (Total tol.)] x 100% = 14.9%

Figure 5.6 Variable data worksheet for example 1 inspection capability study.

The IC evaluation involves combining the repeatability and the reproducibility:

$$SDC = \sqrt{(SDR)^2 + (SDM)^2}$$
$$= \sqrt{(0.0000469)^2 + (0.000016)^2} = 0.0000496$$

Then

$$IC = 6 \times SDC = 6 \times 0.0000496 = 0.000298$$

and

$$PTCC = \frac{IC}{Total\ tolerance} \times 100$$
$$= \frac{0.000298}{0.002} \times 100 = 14.9\%$$

Since the PTCC is 14.9%, the IC of this method is marginally acceptable. Further, since the repeatability is 14% of tolerance and reproducibility is 4.8% of tolerance, corrective action on the gage repeatability is required.

Example 2. An IC study was performed on the measurement of plating thickness using two Dermatron D-9 plating thickness gages and two inspectors. The specification is 0.0002–0.0005 in thick (0.0003 total tolerance).

With two appraisers and two gages, 10 samples with two readings per sample were required according to Table 5.1. The measurements were recorded to the nearest 0.00001 in (the gage increment).

The average range of each appraiser and gage combination is as follows:

Appraiser	Gage	$\bar{R}$
1	A	0.000005
1	B	0.000004
2	A	0.000005
2	B	0.000006

The computations are shown on the worksheet in Fig. 5.7.

The range evaluation is

$$UCL_R = (3.268)(0.000005) = 0.0000163$$

where $D_4 = 3.268$ from Table 5.2 with $n = 2$. Suppose all the ranges are less than the UCL_R.

88   Chapter 5

Variable Data Worksheet

Part number _____ Date _____

Dimension or characteristic ___Plating thickness___

Specification or tolerance ___0.0002 – 0.0005 in. (0.0003 total tolerance)___

1. Range evaluation

| | Original | Revised | Upper control limit range (UCL$_R$) |

$\bar{R}_1$ = 0.000005 _____ $n =$ __2__ D_4 = 3.268

$\bar{R}_2$ = 0.000004 _____   UCL$_R$ = $D_4\bar{R}$ = 0.0000163

$\bar{R}_3$ = 0.000005 _____   No. points above UCL$_R$ = 0

$\bar{R}_4$ = 0.000006 _____   No. points discarded = 0

$\Sigma\bar{R}$ = 0.000020 _____

$\bar{R}$ = 0.000005 _____

2. Repeatability evaluation

SDR = $(1/d_2)\bar{R}$ $n =$ __2__ $1/d_2$ = 0.885

SDR = _____0.0000044_____

Repeatability = 6 x SDR = ___0.0000264___

PTCR = [(6 x SDR) / (Total tol.)] x 100% = 8.8%

3. Reproducibility evaluation ((Appraisers) or Gages)

R_M = $\bar{X}_L - \bar{X}_S$ $\bar{X}_L$ = 0.000330 $\bar{X}_S$ = 0.000325

R_M = 0.000005

SDM = DR_M K = __2__ D = 0.709

SDM = ___0.0000035___

Reproducibility = 6 x SDM = ___0.000021___

PTCM = [(6 x SDM) / (Total tol.)] x 100% = 7% (Appraisers)

Reproducibility evaluation (Appraisers or (Gages))

R_M = $\bar{X}_L - \bar{X}_S$ $\bar{X}_L$ = 0.00033 $\bar{X}_S$ = 0.00032

R_M = 0.00001

SDM = DR_M K = 2 D = 0.709

SDM = ___0.0000071___

Reproducibility = 6 x SDM = ___0.0000426___

PTCM = [(6 x SDM) / (Total tol.)] x 100% = 14.2% (Gages)

4. Inspection capability evaluation

$$SDC = \sqrt{(SDR)^2 + (SDM)^2}$$

↑ Appraisers   ↑ Gages

SDC = ___0.0000091___

PTCC = [(6 x SDC) / (Total tol.)] x 100% = 18.2%

Figure 5.7 Variable data worksheet for example 2 inspection capability study.

The repeatability evaluation is

$$SDR = (0.885)(0.000005) = 0.0000044$$

where $1/d_2 = 0.885$ from Table 5.2 for $n = 2$.
The percent tolerance consumed by repeatability is

$$PTCR = \frac{6 \times 0.0000044}{0.0003} \times 100 = 8.8\%$$

The reproducibility is computed for the appraisers and for the gages. The average of appraiser 1 is 0.000325; for appraiser 2, 0.000330. The range of the appraisers is

$$R_A = 0.000330 - 0.000325 = 0.000005$$

The standard deviation of the appraisers is

$$SDA = DR_A = (0.709)(0.000005) = 0.0000035$$

where $D = 0.709$ from Table 5.4 with $K = 2$ appraisers. The reproducibility of the appraisers is

$$\text{Reproducibility} = 6 \times SDA = 6 \times 0.0000035 = 0.000021$$

The percent tolerance consumed by the appraisers (PTCA) is

$$PTCA = \frac{0.000021}{\text{Total tolerance}} \times 100$$

$$= \frac{0.000021}{0.0003} \times 100 = 7\%$$

The average of gage A is 0.00033; gage B, 0.00032. The range of the gages (R_G) is

$$R_G = 0.00033 - 0.00032 = 0.00001$$

The standard deviation of the gages is

$$SDG = DR_G = (0.709)(0.00001) = 0.0000071$$

where $D = 0.709$ from Table 5.3 with $K = 2$ gages. The reproducibility of the gages is then

$$\text{Reproducibility} = (6)(0.0000071) = 0.0000426$$

The percent tolerance consumed by the gages (PTCG) is

$$PTCG = \frac{0.0000426}{0.0003} \times 100 = 14.2\%$$

To evaluate the IC, we must find SDC, which includes the standard deviation of repeatability plus the standard deviation of reproducibility for both the appraisers and gages.

$$SDC = \sqrt{(SDR)^2 + (SDA)^2 + (SDG)^2}$$

$$= \sqrt{(0.0000044)^2 + (0.0000035)^2 + (0.0000071)^2} = 0.0000091$$

Thus

$$IC = 6SDC = (6)(0.0000091) = 0.0000546$$

and

$$PTCC = \frac{0.0000546}{0.0003} \times 100 = 18.2\%$$

The IC is marginal. The gage reproducibility percent of tolerance is 14.2%. The appraiser reproducibility and repeatability percents of tolerance are both less than 10%. Corrective action must be initiated on the gages due to the lack of gage reproducibility.

Inspection Capability Study for Attribute Data

The concepts of repeatability and reproducibility for attribute data are the same as for variable data, but their measurement is entirely different. The emphasis now is on the capability or effectiveness of the appraiser in detecting conforming or nonconforming parts repeatedly and the degree of his or her bias toward rejecting conforming parts or accepting nonconforming parts. The team can compare the effectiveness of different appraisers when assessing reproducibility.

The following measures are used in the IC study for attribute data:

Effectiveness (E). *Effectiveness* is the ability of an appraiser to accurately detect conforming and nonconforming parts. Effectiveness is expressed as a number between 0 and 1, where 1 is perfection, and is computed as follows:

$$E = \frac{\text{Number of parts correctly identified}}{\text{Total opportunities to be correct}}$$

Total opportunities to be correct is a function of the number of parts used and how many times each part is inspected. If 10 parts are selected and each is inspected 3 times, there are $3 \times 10 = 30$ opportunities to be correct.

Probability of a miss [P(Miss)]. The *probability of a miss* is the chance of not rejecting a nonconforming part. This error is serious because a nonconforming part is accepted. Mathematically,

$$P(\text{Miss}) = \frac{\text{Number of misses}}{\text{Number of opportunities for a miss}}$$

The number of opportunities for a miss is a function of the number of nonconforming parts used in the study and the number of times each part is inspected. If 5 nonconforming parts are used and each part is inspected 3 times, then there are $3 \times 5 = 15$ opportunities for a miss.

Probability of a false alarm [$P(\text{FA})$]. The *probability of a false alarm* is the chance of rejecting a conforming part. This type of error is not as serious as a miss. However, rejecting a conforming part causes rework and reinspection when they are unnecessary. If $P(\text{FA})$ gets too large, the wasteful cost of rework and reinspection dramatically increases. Mathematically,

$$P(\text{FA}) = \frac{\text{Number of false alarms}}{\text{Number of opportunities for a false alarm}}$$

The number of opportunities for a false alarm is a function of the number of conforming parts used in the study and the number of times each part is inspected. If 6 conforming parts are used and each part is inspected 3 times, then there are $3 \times 6 = 18$ opportunities for a false alarm.

Bias (B). *Bias* is a measure of a person's tendency to classify an item as conforming or nonconforming, and is a function of $P(\text{Miss})$ and $P(\text{FA})$. Bias values are equal to or greater than 0 and have the following meanings:

$B = 1$ implies no bias.

$B > 1$ implies bias toward rejecting parts.

$B < 1$ implies bias toward accepting parts.

Bias is computed by the formula

$$B = B(\text{FA})/B(\text{Miss})$$

where $B(\text{FA})$ is a factor found in Table 5.5 and is a function of $P(\text{FA})$, and $B(\text{Miss})$ is also a factor found in Table 5.5 and is a function of $P(\text{Miss})$.

Example. Suppose an IC study involving attribute data is conducted. Suppose further that $P(\text{FA}) = 0.04$ and $P(\text{Miss}) = 0.17$. The factor from Table 5.5 corresponding to $P(\text{FA})$ is $B(\text{FA}) = 0.0863$, and the factor corresponding to $P(\text{Miss})$ is $B(\text{Miss}) = 0.2541$. The bias value B is then

$$B = 0.0863/0.2541 = 0.34$$

TABLE 5.5 Bias Factor Table for Inspection Capability Studies Involving
Attribute Data

$P(FA)$ or $P(Miss)$	$B(FA)$ or $B(Miss)$	$P(FA)$ or $P(Miss)$	$B(FA)$ or $B(Miss)$
0.01	0.0264	0.26	0.3251
0.02	0.0488	0.27	0.3312
0.03	0.0681	0.28	0.3372
0.04	0.0863	0.29	0.3429
0.05	0.1040	0.30	0.3485
0.06	0.1200	0.31	0.3538
0.07	0.1334	0.32	0.3572
0.08	0.1497	0.33	0.3621
0.09	0.1626	0.34	0.3668
0.10	0.1758	0.35	0.3712
0.11	0.1872	0.36	0.3739
0.12	0.1989	0.37	0.3778
0.13	0.2107	0.38	0.3814
0.14	0.2227	0.39	0.3836
0.15	0.2323	0.40	0.3867
0.16	0.2444	0.41	0.3885
0.17	0.2541	0.42	0.3910
0.18	0.2613	0.43	0.3925
0.19	0.2709	0.44	0.3945
0.20	0.2803	0.45	0.3961
0.21	0.2874	0.46	0.3970
0.22	0.2966	0.47	0.3977
0.23	0.3034	0.48	0.3984
0.24	0.3101	0.49	0.3989
0.25	0.3187	0.50	0.3989

This value indicates a strong bias toward accepting parts and is an
unacceptable condition. Table 5.6 lists special cases encountered in
computing the bias value when $P(FA)$ or $P(Miss)$ are zero or greater
than 0.50.

Data collection for attribute data

Collecting samples for evaluating an IC study with attribute data is
quite different from collecting samples for variable data. The parts are
not selected at random but are selected by knowledgeable personnel
(supervisor or engineer) and must be evaluated as conforming or
nonconforming. The recommended number of parts to be selected is
shown in Table 5.7. The parts are selected so that there will be one-
third conforming, one-third nonconforming, and one-third marginal.
The marginal parts are further divided so that half are marginally

TABLE 5.6 Special Cases in Computing Bias

$P(FA)$	$P(Miss)$	B	Decision or action
0	More than 0	0	Unacceptable
More than 0	0	No value	Use E, $P(FA)$, and $P(Miss)$ directly
0	0	No value	This is same as $B = 1$ since $P(FA) = P(Miss)$; acceptable
More than 0.5	0.5 or less	More than 1.5	Unacceptable
0.5 or less	More than 0.5	Less than 0.5	Unacceptable
More than 0.5	More than 0.5	No value	Bias unimportant; study is unacceptable based on $P(Miss)$ and $P(FA)$ being more than 0.5

conforming and half are marginally nonconforming. Thus the total sample is half conforming parts and half nonconforming parts.

After the parts are selected they are inspected once in a random order by each inspector, and the results are recorded on data sheets. The inspection is repeated by each inspector, and the results are recorded on separate data sheets to eliminate any unintentional bias. Inspections are repeated until the required number is completed.

Data analysis for attribute data

The team analyzes the data using the appropriate worksheets to compute $P(Miss)$, $P(FA)$, E, and B. The analysis will be illustrated by the following example.

Example. This example is concerned with a plating operation on a computer printer part. Visual inspection detects stains and deposits on the part after plating. Three persons were involved in the study: the plating operator, the inspector, and the lead inspector. Seventeen parts were selected initially, and, after evaluation of the samples by the quality engineer, manufacturing engineer, and inspection supervisor, 14 parts (8 conforming and 6 nonconforming) were actually used in the study. Each part was inspected three times. The data obtained are

TABLE 5.7 Sample Sizes for Inspection Capability Studies Involving Attribute Data

Number of appraisers	Minimum number of parts	Minimum number of inspections per part
1	24	5
2	18	4
3 or more	12	3

shown in Table 5.8. The column marked C or N contains the true condition of the part, where C means conforming or acceptable and N means nonconforming or rejected.

The analysis consists mainly of counting and division. We will use the attribute data worksheet in Fig. 5.8 to describe the details of the computations.

Inspection results

Column 1: Good correct. Column 1 is the number of good or conforming parts identified correctly by the person inspecting the parts. Since there are 8 conforming parts each inspected 3 times, 24 opportunities exist for correct identification of the conforming parts for each person. Appraiser A correctly identified the conforming parts 19 times. Part assemblies 1, 4, 10, 13, 14, and 16 were all accepts (18 total), while assembly 8 had no accepts and assembly 9 had 1 accept.

Column 2: Bad correct. Column 2 is the number of bad or nonconforming parts identified correctly by the person inspecting these parts. Since there are 6 nonconforming parts each inspected 3 times, 18 opportunities exist for correct identification of the nonconforming parts for each person. Appraiser A correctly identified the nonconforming parts all 18 times.

Column 3: Total correct. Column 3 is the sum of columns (1) and (2) and is the numerator of the formula for computing E.

TABLE 5.8 Data for Attribute Data Analysis Example

Assembly	C or N	Appraiser A			Appraiser B			Appraiser C		
		1	2	3	1	2	3	1	2	3
1	C	C	C	C	C	C	C	C	C	C
3	N	N	N	N	N	N	N	N	N	N
4	C	C	C	C	C	C	C	C	C	C
5	N	N	N	N	N	N	N	N	N	N
6	N	N	N	N	N	C	N	N	N	N
8	C	N	N	N	C	C	C	C	C	C
9	C	N	C	N	C	C	C	C	N	C
10	C	C	C	C	C	C	C	C	C	C
11	N	N	N	N	C	C	C	C	C	C
13	C	C	C	C	C	C	C	C	C	C
14	C	C	C	C	C	C	C	C	C	C
15	N	N	N	N	N	N	N	N	N	N
16	C	C	C	C	C	C	C	C	C	C
17	N	N	N	N	N	N	N	N	N	N

Attribute Data Worksheet

Part number _____ Date _____

Inspection instruction no. _____ Revision _____ Date _____

Characteristics inspected _____ Stains and deposits _____

Inspection results

Appraiser	Good correct (1)	Bad correct (2)	Total correct (3)	False alarms (4)	Misses (5)	Grand total (6)
A	19	18	37	5	0	42
B	24	14	38	0	4	42
C	23	15	38	1	3	42

Calculations

Appraiser	E $[(3)/(6)]$	$P(\text{FA})$ $((4)/[(1)+(4)])$	$P(\text{Miss})$ $((5)/[(2)+(5)])$	Bias $[B(\text{FA})/B(\text{Miss})]$
A	37/42 = 0.88	5/24 = 0.21	0/18 = 0	
B	38/42 = 0.90	0/24 = 0	4/18 = 0.22	0
C	38/42 = 0.90	1/29 = 0.04	3/18 = 0.17	0.34

Figure 5.8 Attribute data worksheet example.

Column 4: False alarms.   Column 4 is the number of false alarms (FA) for each person. Appraiser A had five false alarms, three on assembly 8 and one on assembly 9.

Column 5: Misses.   Column 5 is the number of misses for each person. Appraiser A had no misses. Appraiser B had four misses: one on assembly 6 and three on assembly 11.

Column 6: Grand total.   Column 6 is the sum of columns 3–5 and should equal the number of parts inspected times the number of inspections per part. In the example, 14 parts were inspected 3 times for a total of 42.

Calculations

$E = (3)/(6)$.   Effectiveness (E) is the value in column (3) divided by the value in column (6) for each appraiser. For appraiser A, $E = 37/42 = 0.88$.

$P(\text{FA}) = (4)/[(1) + (4)]$.   The probability of a false alarm [$P(\text{FA})$] is the value in column (4) divided by the sum of the values in columns (1) and (4). The sum of columns (1) and (4) is the number of opportunities for false alarms, which is the same as the number of opportunities for correctly identifying the conforming parts (24 in this example). For appraiser A, $P(\text{FA}) = 5/(19 + 5) = 5/24 = 0.21$.

$P(\text{Miss}) = (5)/[(2) + (5)]$.   The probability of a miss [$P(\text{Miss})$] is the value in column (5) divided by the sum of the values in columns (2) and (5). The sum of columns (2) and (5) is the number of opportunities for misses, which is the same as the number of opportunities for correctly identifying the nonconforming parts (18 in this example). For appraiser B, $P(\text{Miss}) = 4/(14 + 4) = 0.22$.

Bias $= B(\text{FA})/B(\text{Miss})$.   This column computes the bias value for each appraiser. Appraiser A has $P(\text{Miss}) = 0$, which gives no value for the bias, as described previously. Appraiser B has $P(\text{FA}) = 0$, which gives a bias of 0, as described previously. For appraiser C, $P(\text{Miss}) = 0.17$ and $P(\text{FA}) = 0.04$. From Table 5.5, $B(\text{Miss}) = 0.2541$ and $B(\text{FA}) = 0.0863$. Thus $B = 0.0863/0.2541 = 0.34$, which indicates bias toward accepting parts.

Data evaluation for attribute data

The overall IC study is evaluated by the team using Table 5.9, based on the four computed measures E, $P(\text{FA})$, $P(\text{Miss})$, and B. For any marginally acceptable or unacceptable gages or appraisers, corrective action is required. When the corrective action is completed, the IC study should be redone.

TABLE 5.9   Evaluation Criteria for Inspection Capability Studies Involving Attribute
Data

Parameter	Acceptable	Marginal	Unacceptable
E	0.9 or more	0.8–0.9	Less than 0.8
$P(FA)$	0.05 or less	0.05–0.10	More than 0.10
$P(Miss)$	0.02 or less	0.02–0.05	More than 0.05
B	0.80–1.20	0.50–0.80 or 1.2–1.5	Less than 0.50 or more than 1.5

Reporting the Results

Reporting the results of an IC study provides a record of the details
and results. Following are some guidelines for writing the report.
(Before conducting the study, the team should prepare a report for
review by the steering committee, which contains the purpose and methodology sections only. This report allows the members of the team and
the steering committee to become familiar with the details of the study
and the resources (time, material, and equipment required.) The report
consists of six sections:

1. *Purpose.*   A brief statement of the reasons for, and the scope of, the
   study. This is the objective statement of the study and should identify the number of gages, operators, or machines that will be
   involved.

2. *Findings and conclusions.*   This section summarizes the results. The
   capability should be stated as acceptable, marginally acceptable, or
   unacceptable. The values of percent tolerance consumed, $P(Miss)$,
   B, and other appropriate measures should be given in tabular form.

3. *Recommendations.*   This section indicates what should be done
   about a marginal or unacceptable study. The recommendations
   should be supported by the findings and conclusions. Resources
   required to implement the recommendations should be identified,
   along with the person responsible for implementation and the
   expected completion dates. The CP action worksheet in Fig. 5.9
   should be used to summarize the above items.

4. *Methodology.*   This section explains what was done and how the data
   were collected, including all details and assumptions.

5. *Analysis and data.*   This section contains the data and calculation
   details. Any worksheets that were used should be in this section.
   The summary, data recording sheets, data worksheets, and checklists must be used to present the data.

Inspection Capability Study
Corrective and Preventive Action Worksheet

Part number: _____   Date: _____

Part name: _____   Quality engineer: _____

Specification or tolerance: _____   Inspector: _____

Study disposition:

CP action	Responsibility	Target date	Completion date

Figure 5.9 CP action worksheet for IC study.

6. *Discussion.* This section contains further supporting information and descriptions of unusual occurrences.

7. *Distribution.* Copies go to team members, the team leader, the steering committee, supervisors, and the quality engineering file.

Checklist

The checklist in Fig. 5.10 helps the team design, conduct, analyze, and report on IC study. It also helps the steering committee determine if the team covered all points.

SUMMARY

The IC study is a method for evaluating an inspection or measurement system for variable and attribute data. The IC measurement for variable data is a percent of total tolerance. The measurement of IC for visual or attribute data involves four values: $P(\text{Miss})$, $P(\text{FA})$, E (effectiveness), and B (bias).

An IC study must be performed before conducting a process capability study to be sure that an accurate measurement or inspection method is in place. This is a critical element in successfully implementing SPC in the PQI process.

After the team has performed an IC study and found acceptable results or performed the corrective action to obtain an acceptable IC, it can move ahead to further analysis of the process in step 6 (Chap. 6) by conducting a process capability study.

Inspection Capability Study Checklist			
Item	Description	Findings (acceptable, marginal, unacceptable)	Action required
1.0	Study Preparation and Design		
1.1	Is the purpose or objective stated?		
1.2	Is the type of data (variable or attribute) identified?		
1.3	Does an inspection instruction exist? Number _____ Revision _____		
1.3.1	Does the method reflect current practice?		
1.4	How many appraisers are to be involved?		
1.5	How many gages or pieces of test equipment are involved?		
1.6	Is a data collection method/procedure prepared and available?		
1.6.1	What is the sample size?		
1.6.2	How many inspections or measurements per sample are required?		
1.6.3	Does the order for inspection or measurement of the samples follow the method described in the section "Data collection for variable data" in Chap.5?		
1.6.4	Are there any special conditions (test method restrictions, etc.) that will affect the data collection?		
1.6.5	Is the study to be conducted in the same location as it is performed every day?		
1.6.6	Are the inspection measurement conditions (lighting, inspection time, inspection location) the same as those in current use?		
1.6.7	If there are any exceptions, how are they being compensated for in the analysis and interpretation?		
1.6.8	Is there a data recording form?		
1.6.9	Is the form acceptable?		
1.7	Has a plan with a purpose and a data collection method been issued?		
1.7.1	Has the plan been approved by the appropriate manager?		
1.7.2	Has the plan been approved by the steering committee?		
2.0	Data Collection		
2.1	Have the samples been obtained and identified with a number or code?		
2.2	Were samples, including those out of specification, for variable data selected at random?		

Figure 5.10 IC study checklist.

Item	Description	Findings (acceptable, marginal, unacceptable)	Action required
2.3	Is the sample for attribute data composed of 1/3 acceptable, 1/3 marginal (composed of 1/2 marginally acceptable and 1/2 marginally unacceptable), and 1/3 unacceptable parts? (This results in about 1/2 of the samples being acceptable.)		
2.3.1	Were the samples for attribute data selected by QE and the QC supervisor?		
2.3.2	Are the defects on the samples selected an element on the inspection instructions?		
2.3.3	Are any defects omitted? Why were they omitted?		
2.4	Has the purpose of the study and data collection method been reviewed with participants?		
2.5	Has the inspection method been reviewed with the appraisers?		
2.6	Have the roles of the participants been explained?		
3.0	Data Analysis		
3.1	Variable data		
3.1.1	Is the average range equal to or greater than 0?		
3.1.2	Was the correct D_4 factor used for UCL_R?		
3.1.3	Are any ranges above UCL_R?		
3.1.4	What action is being done if any ranges are above UCL_R?		
3.1.5	Is the repeatability computed correctly?		
3.1.6	Is reproducibility computed correctly?*		
3.1.7	Is the overall inspection capability computed correctly?		
3.1.8	Are both appraisers and gages included, if used, in the capability computation?		
3.1.9	Is the result acceptable, marginal or unacceptable?		
3.2	Attribute data		
3.2.1	Are the number of conforming parts accepted counted correctly?		
3.2.2	Are the number of nonconforming parts rejected counted correctly?		
3.2.3	Are the number of conforming parts rejected (false alarms) counted correctly?		
3.2.4	Are the number of nonconforming parts accepted (misses) counted correctly?		

Figure 5.10 (*Continued*)

Item	Description	Findings (acceptable, marginal, unacceptable)	Action required
3.2.5	Have the computations been checked for E, P (Miss), P (FA), and B ?		
3.2.6	Is the result acceptable,marginal, or unacceptable?		
4.0	Reporting Results		
4.1	Has the report containing the results of the study been written and issued?		
4.2	Does the report follow report guidelines?		
4.3	Does the report contain purpose,findings and conclusions, recommendations, methodology, and data analysis sections?		
4.4	Has the report been reviewed and approved by the appropriate manager?		
5.0	Preventive Action		
5.1	Is any preventive action required (marginal and unacceptable studies)?		
5.2	Has preventive action been assigned, using the corrective and preventive action matrix, to the responsible station?		
5.3	If preventive action is required, when will the inspection capability study be repeated?		

*The computation of reproducibility of appraisers is required if more than one appraiser is used; the computation of reproducibility of gages is required if more than one gage is used.

Figure 5.10 (*Continued*)

6

Process Capability*

In the last chapter the team discovered problems or inadequacies in the inspection system and used the problem-solving techniques to resolve them.Thus the inspection system is now acceptable and capable of consistent output. The team can now thoroughly evaluate the process it is addressing.

A quality product can be made only when the production processes are able to consistently meet specific targets. When processes cannot meet these requirements, cost is added to the product in the form of scrap, rework, or both. This chapter describes step 6 of the PQI process, process capability. A *process capability study* is a procedure for evaluating a process by means of control charts (refer to Chap. 9) to determine if the process is capable relative to its specifications and the centering and stability (see p. 113) of the process. The study also determines if the process is behaving naturally or unnaturally, investigates the causes of any unnatural behavior, and recommends the action necessary to eliminate any disturbances. Specifically a process capability study can

- Improve productivity and quality
- Determine the design tolerances that can be met with the current processes
- Determine if new equipment is capable of meeting the requirements
- Compare the process capabilities of different equipment and machines

---

*Wendell Paulson participated in preparing this chapter.

Normally it is not feasible to determine process capability by direct measurements of process or machine operating conditions. Instead the output of the process is measured to determine the natural process variation. Such a study may involve a single process (simple or complex) or a sequence of processes (production sequence). In its simplest form, a machine capability study, the study involves a single operation (machine) and one person (operator). The team conducts a machine capability study under normal operating conditions while holding constant as many variables as possible, usually by obtaining consecutive pieces for a short time with no adjustments or material changes. This method allows a measure of the inherent or natural process variation while using the fewest samples and least amount of time. It is a single-level design of experiments, where time is the variable. Examples of natural process variation are tool wear, operator-initiated machine adjustments, material variation, and equipment wear.

As mentioned, process capability is the inherent or natural variation of a process after undesirable disturbances are eliminated. The capability for a process involving variable data is expressed as six times the value of the standard deviation, or 6σ. This number is compared to the requirement by a capability ratio, which is 6σ divided by the total tolerance. Multiplying this number by 100 gives the percent tolerance consumed by the capability. The capability for a process involving attribute data is simply the average value or center line of the control chart.

Several indexes for quantifying the capability of a process involving variable data have been developed. Some of the more commonly used ones are Cpk, Cp, Zmin, CPU, and CPL. The Zmin, CPU, and CPL indexes also include the location of the process average relative to the specification nominal. These indexes are being used by many large corporations such as Ford, GM, and Xerox as a requirement for the supplier's processes. The calculations for these indexes can be found in many texts.

This chapter discusses how to design the process capability study, conduct the study, and analyze and evaluate variable and attribute data results. A process capability study checklist (Fig. 6.1) is used by the team to be sure that all items are considered during the study.

Process Capability Study Design

The design of a capability study includes review of current methods, defining the scope of the study, and developing data collection methods.

		Findings (acceptable, marginal,	
Item	Description	unacceptable)	Action required
1.0	Designing the Study		
1.1	What dimensions and characteristics are to be studied?		
1.2	What type of data will be obtained, variable or attribute?		
1.3	How many machines are included?		
1.4	How many operators are included?		
1.5	Does this process run on two shifts?		
1.6	Are both shifts to be included in the study?		
1.7	What is the production rate (min/piece, pieces/hr)?		
1.8	What are the number and revision of the manufacturing method?		
1.9	Does the manufacturing method reflect current practice?		
1.10	Fabrication process review		
1.10.1	What are the machine settings (speeds, feeds, temperatures)?		
1.10.2	What type of process will be used, cut, grind, drill, ream, or another process?		
1.10.3	Is the work done on a single or multiple spindle/fixture operation?		
1.10.4	How is the part located?		
1.10.5	Are adjustments manual or automatic?		
1.10.6	How long is the operation cycle?		
1.11	Assembly process review		
1.11.1	How is the part located?		
1.11.2	Is the assembly manual or automatic?		
1.11.3	Are adjustments manual or automatic?		
1.11.4	How long is the operation cycle?		
1.12	What are the number and revision of the inspection instruction?		
1.13	Has the inspection capability study been performed?		
1.14	Were the results acceptable?		
1.15	If the inspection capability was marginal or unacceptable, is corrective action complete?		
1.16	Was the inspection capability study redone?		
1.17	Was the redone study accepted?		

Process Capability Study Checklist

Figure 6.1 Process capability study checklist.

Item	Description	Findings (acceptable, marginal, unacceptable)	Action required
1.18	Have any noted exceptions been resolved?		
1.19	Inspection instruction review		
1.19.1	How are the dimensions or characteristics to be studied, measured, or inspected?		
1.19.2	Does the inspection instruction reflect current practice?		
1.20	Data collection method		
1.20.1	Has the data collection method been written?		
1.20.2	Is it approved (QE, steering committee)?		
1.20.3	Have size, number, and frequency of subgroups been specified?		
1.20.4	Are consecutive pieces being grouped into subgroups or are subgroups being collected periodically?		
1.20.5	How are the parts being marked to determine the order of production?		
1.20.6	Are parts to be measured in the same order as they are made?		
1.20.7	What will be done to assure that the parts are collected prior to any screening or corrections by the operator or inspector?		
1.20.8	What will be done to assure that the parts are collected properly during the study?		
1.20.9	Who will monitor the data collection?		
1.20.10	Are parts to be produced under normal operating conditions (lighting, temperatures, pressures, speeds, feeds, materials)?		
1.20.11	If there are any exceptions to normal conditions, how are they being compensated for in the results?		
1.20.12	Have data recording forms been developed?		
1.20.13	Are the forms complete?		
1.20.14	Are the forms easy to use?		
1.20.15	Have the data collection responsibilities of the participants been defined?		
1.20.16	Has a preliminary report containing the purpose, objective, scope, and data collection method been issued?		
1.20.17	Is the report approved?		
2.0	Conducting the Study		
2.1	Is the measuring equipment calibrated?		
2.2	Are trained operators selected?		

Figure 6.1   (*Continued*)

Item	Description	Findings (acceptable, marginal, unacceptable)	Action required
2.3	Did the selected inspector have acceptable results in the inspection capability study?		
2.4	Has the study been described to the operators, inspectors, and supervisors?		
2.5	Were the first pieces submitted for inspection and approved?		
2.6	Is adequate material on hand to perform the study?		
2.7	Has an events log been posted to record any changes that may occur during the study?		
2.8	Will the parts be saved?		
2.9	Will QE and ME be present during the study to monitor the data collection?		
2.10	Are the data recording forms being used?		
2.11	Did a major process or machine breakdown occur during the study? If so, when is the study rescheduled?		
3.0	Analyzing and Interpreting Data		
3.1	Were the data plotted on the appropriate control chart?		
3.2	Were the center lines and control limits computed?		
3.3	Were the capability values computed (PTCC for variable data, center line for attribute data)?		
3.4	Were the capability values computed for a control chart with out-of-control points?		
3.5	For variable data, were any ranges out of control? What was done?		
4.0	Evaluation of Results		
4.1	Has the study been evaluated as acceptable, marginal, or unacceptable?		
4.2	For marginal or unacceptable studies, have the corrective actions been identified and assigned completion dates?		
4.3	Is the study to be repeated when the corrective actions are complete?		
5.0	Reporting Results		
5.1	Is a report being prepared containing the results of the study?		
5.2	When will the report be issued?		
5.3	Does the report contain the purpose, findings and conclusions, recommendations, methodology, and data analysis details?		

Figure 6.1 (*Continued*)

Review of current methods

The first action taken by the team in the design phase is to review current manufacturing and inspection methods.

Manufacturing methods. When reviewing the manufacturing method, the team follows these procedures:

1. It must become familiar with the part and how it is actually made or assembled
2. It must determine the part's features or characteristics that will be used in the study and identify these characteristics as variable or attribute
3. If a fabrication process is being studied, the team determines
   a. The type of fabrication being used (e.g., cut, grind, drill, ream, punch, or form)
   b. The number of machines or redundant cause-systems to be studied
   c. If a single- or multiple-spindle machine or single- or multiple-fixture machine is being used
   d. If the adjustments are automatic or manual
   e. The operation cycle time
   f. The machine or process settings, such as speed, feed, pressure, or temperature
   g. The number of machines and operators used and how many shifts the process runs
4. If an assembly process is being studied, the team
   a. Reviews the documented assembly method to determine if it is current and reflects current practices
   b. Determine if a fixture (if one is used) is the latest configuration and if it properly locates the part
   c. Determines the assembly operation cycle time
   d. Determines how many operators and fixtures are used and the number of shifts
   e. Determines if equipment used is in calibration

Inspection method. The team should review the inspection method to become familiar with the way the product is measured, inspected, or tested, by

1. Reviewing the documented inspection method.
2. Determining how the part is measured, inspected, or tested.
3. Reviewing the IC study. If the results were marginal or unacceptable, the team must determine if corrective actions have been completed, if the study has then been redone, and if results are now acceptable. If the IC study has not been performed or is still marginal

or unacceptable, the process capability study should be deferred until an acceptable IC study has been performed.

Defining the scope of the capability study

Defining the scope of the capability study means identifying those items to be included in the study. The team should:

1. Select the characteristics to be studied. As many as possible should be studied, since the process capability can be determined for each characteristic studied from the same set of parts. If six characteristics are measured on a part, six process capability studies can be completed at the same time.

2. Determine the characteristics to be studied and which will be variable data and which will be attribute data.

3. Determine the number of machines or assembly operations to be studied. (A study is usually performed on each machine or assembly operation.)

4. Determine the number of people (operators and inspectors) to be included. Usually only one person is studied at a time. If a study encompasses two machines and two operators and if the operators influence the operation, then four studies are required (one for each machine and operator combination) for a full process evaluation. If the machine has automatic settings, then one operator can be selected at random and used for a study on each machine. One person, trained and capable, should be chosen to do the inspecting or measuring.

5. Determine how a multiple-shift process will be handled. A separate study is usually performed on each shift, or notes are made on the events log or control chart when shift changes occur.

6. Determine what adjustments the operator is allowed to make. (The goal is to minimize adjustments.) Adjustments are sometimes made because the company has always made them. This situation is especially true if the process involves tool wear as in a cutting or grinding operation. For example, a manufacturing method called for adjusting a grinding wheel every 200 parts. The adjustment took 15 to 20 minutes, resulting in a significant production loss. The rationale for the adjustments was that it was company practice. During the process capability study the team decided to make no adjustments to the grinding wheel so that its capability could be determined. The result was that 1200 parts could be machined before the wheel needed adjusting. Thus, six adjustment delays were omitted and 90 to 120 minutes of productivity were added.

In summary, a process capability study should be conducted under normal operating conditions with a single batch of raw material, a single operator, and a single inspector while the data are collected. The operator should not correct the process or make adjustments during the study. Measuring equipment should not be calibrated unless inspection instructions are specified.

Developing data collection methods

Developing data collection methods includes determining the number of samples to be collected, deciding how the samples are to be obtained and collected, and designing the data collection form.

Number of samples. The sample size required for a capability study can range from 25 to 1250 pieces and is related to the method of analysis to be used. Normal probability paper requires a minimum of 25 consecutive pieces. $\bar{X}$ and R control charts require 25 subgroups of 5 samples (125 total samples); more than 25 subgroups are required in order to determine the effects of material, operators, and machine wear over time. p charts require 25 subgroups of 50 samples (1250 total samples), and c charts require 25 subgroups of 1 to 5 samples (25 to 125 total samples).

The guidelines for variable data subgroup selection (size and frequency) are a function of production volume. For high volume (50 or more parts per hour) select a subgroup of consecutive pieces every 15 to 30 minutes or every 25–30 pieces produced. For low volume (less than 50 parts per hour) select subgroups of four or five consecutive pieces: for example, if subgroups of 5 are used and consecutive pieces are grouped into subgroups, the first 5 pieces are subgroup 1, pieces 6 to 10 are subgroup 2, etc.

Attribute data are collected and analyzed with the help of the appropriate attribute control chart. At least 25 subgroups are required, and the frequency is a function of the production rate, similar to the variable data study. For high volume (50 or more parts per hour) collect subgroups every 15 to 30 minutes or every 25 or 50 pieces. If a p chart or np chart is used, consecutive pieces may have to be used, with every 25 or 50 pieces constituting a subgroup. For low volume (less than 50 parts per hour) use consecutive pieces and break into subgroups.

A process capability study with attribute data can be performed using the results of 100% inspection, provided an acceptable IC study has been done. The subgroup size is often the number of parts inspected during a shift or day, which frequently gives unequal subgroup sizes.

Sample selection. Samples are to be selected from the process before any rework or sorting occurs. It is imperative that the operator not select the parts.

Data collection forms.   Forms that allow data to be recorded quickly and easily must be designed.

Conducting the Study

Conducting the study consists primarily of data collection. In order to collect the data properly, the team must prepare both the process and the people.

Preparing the process

The team must

1. Review the IC study. An *acceptable* IC study is required before the process capability study is done.
2. Calibrate the measuring equipment.
3. Set up the machine or process under normal conditions. Ensure that the normal environment and materials are used. (New materials or methods should not be used. Additional studies are required to evaluate the new materials or methods and should be conducted at another time.)
4. Have the first samples inspected and accepted by an inspector. The study must not be run until the first pieces are produced to specification.
5. Initiate an events log to record anything new, different, or changed during the study. (If it is a new events log the first entry might be that a process capability study is being conducted.)

Preparing the people

The team must

1. Select a trained operator and inspector. Normally only one operator is involved unless the process is operator dependent. One inspector is normally used throughout a study, one who has achieved an acceptable IC study.
2. Discuss the study with the operator(s) and inspector(s). Describe the purpose of the study and provide a detailed explanation of the data collection and data recording methods.
3. Explain the role of the operator. Explain the adjustments that the operator is allowed to make during the study. One of the main functions of the operator is to record any changes to the process in the events log.

4. Explain the role of the inspector. The inspector identifies, measures, and inspects the parts, and records the data on the data collection form. It is important that the order in which the parts are produced be recorded (identify them with a number). Typically in a process capability study, all parts are collected before any measurements are made. Thus the identification of parts is important for creating subgroups and analyzing results. The measurement of the parts can be in random order or in the same order as the parts were made, whichever is easier.

When the data are being collected, the people who designed the study must be present to audit the data collection procedure to ensure that the data collection follows the plan. They should

1. Record all pertinent information in the events log, including the date, operator, inspector, machine or operation number, process conditions (speed, pressures, temperature), and characteristics being checked.

2. Ensure that any changes in the process during the study are recorded in the events log along with the time the event occurred.

3. Save all parts that were measured or inspected until the data evaluation is completed (in case measurements or inspections must be repeated due to freak readings).

Analyzing and Evaluating the Results

The method of data analysis and evaluation depends on the control chart used to collect the data. The following sections describe the analysis and evaluation for the variable control chart ($\overline{X}$ and R chart) and the attribute control charts. [If normal probability paper is used (25–30 consecutive samples), see Chap. 12 of *Quality Planning and Analysis* by Joseph M. Juran and Frank M. Gryna, Jr., for a discussion of the analysis.]

Variable data

This section contains the details of the analysis and evaluation of a process capability study using an $\overline{X}$ and R chart.

Analysis. Plot the subgroup data on an $\overline{X}$ and R chart. Compute the center line ($\overline{R}$) and control limits for the R chart. If the R chart is in control, compute the limits for the $\overline{X}$ chart. (Formulas for computing the center line and control limits are in Chap. 12 of *Quality Planning and Analysis* or Chap. 4 of *Statistical Quality Control* by Eugene L.

Grant and Richard Leavenworth.) If the R chart is not in control, use the following guidelines to evaluate the results:

1. For any subgroup range exceeding the upper control limit (UCL_R), remeasure the part to determine if there is an error in measuring the part or in recording the data. If there is a measurement or data recording error, replace the reading and recalculate. If more than one range exceeds the UCL_R due to measurement errors, then review the IC again and redo the study.

2. Subgroup ranges that are more than 10 times the average range are considered wild or freak readings. If only one subgroup is affected, remove the reading. Otherwise, there may be a major problem affecting the variation of the process. Develop and initiate the appropriate corrective action, and redo the study after the corrective action is completed.

Evaluation. The evaluation of the process capability study is concerned with variation, stability, and centering of the process. The *variation* of the process is compared to the specification by computing the capability ratio (C_r) as follows:

$$C_r = 6\sigma/\text{Total tolerance}$$

where total tolerance = USL − LSL.

$$6\sigma = 6\,\bar{R}/d_2$$

where $\bar{R}$ is the average range and d_2 is a factor from Table 6.1. Multiply the capability ratio by 100 to give the percent tolerance consumed by the capability (PTCC).

The *stability* of the process is concerned with the process average. If the $\bar{X}$ chart is in control, the process average is considered stable.

The *centering* of the process is concerned with where the process average is with respect to the specification nominal. If the specification nominal is within the control limits for the averages, then the process average is considered not significantly different from the specification nominal.

The criteria for whether a process capability study is acceptable, marginal, or unacceptable are shown in Table 6.2. The criteria evaluate variability, stability, and centering. Determine and initiate corrective action if the process capability is marginal or unacceptable. Use the corrective and preventive action matrix, Fig. 7.2 in the next chapter, to define what actions are to be taken, who is to carry them out, and when they are to be done. When the actions are completed, repeat the process capability study to determine if the actions were effective.

TABLE 6.1   a. $\bar{X}$ and R Control Chart Factors. b. Formulas for Computing Control Limits.

a

Subgroup or sample size	Average	Range		σ
n	A_2	D_3	D_4	d_2
2	1.880	0	3.268	1.128
3	1.023	0	2.574	1.693
4	0.729	0	2.282	2.059
5	0.577	0	2.114	2.326
6	0.483	0	2.004	2.534
7	0.419	0.076	1.924	2.704
8	0.373	0.135	1.854	2.847
9	0.337	0.184	1.816	2.970
10	0.308	0.223	1.777	3.078
11	0.285	0.256	1.744	3.173
12	0.266	0.284	1.717	3.258
13	0.249	0.308	1.692	3.336
14	0.235	0.329	1.671	3.407
15	0.223	0.348	1.652	3.472

b

Average	Range	σ
$\text{UCL} = \bar{\bar{X}} + A_2\bar{R}$ $\text{LCL} = \bar{\bar{X}} - A_2\bar{R}$	$\text{UCL}_R = D_4\bar{R}$ $\text{LCL}_R = D_3\bar{R}$	$\sigma = \dfrac{\bar{R}}{d_2}$

TABLE 6.2   Evaluation Criteria for Process Capability Studies Involving Variable Data

C_r	$\bar{X}$ chart in control?	Specification nominal within control limits on $\bar{X}$ chart?	Decision
75% or less	Yes	Yes	Acceptable
	Yes	No	Marginal
	No	Yes	Marginal
	No	No	Unacceptable
75–100%	Yes	Yes	Marginal
	Yes	No	Marginal
	No	Yes	Marginal
	No	No	Unacceptable
100% or more	Not applicable	Not applicable	Unacceptable

Example. Suppose a process capability study was conducted on a punch-press operation. One of the characteristics of major interest is the width of a slot having a specification of 0.4040 units ± 0.007 units. Twenty-five subgroups of five pieces were obtained during a shift, and the results are shown in Fig. 6.2. Determine if the process is capable of meeting the specification.

From the average ($\overline{X}$) and range (R) charts in Fig. 6.2, note that the R chart is in control. Thus the 6σ of the process can be determined:

$$6\sigma = 6\,\overline{R}/d_2$$

$\overline{R}$, the average range, is 0.004 and $d_2 = 2.326$ from Table 6.1. Thus

$$6\sigma = 6 \times 0.004/2.326 = 6 \times 0.00172 = 0.01032$$

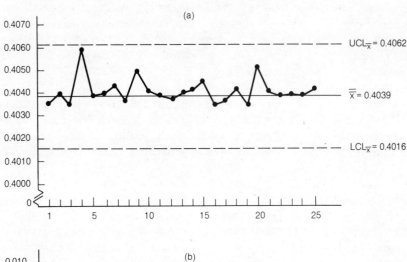

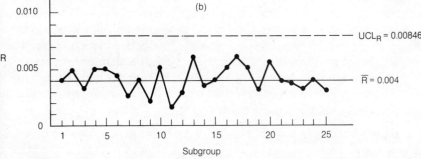

Figure 6.2 Control chart for a punch-press process, showing slot width. (a) X chart. (b) R chart. (UCL stands for upper control limit, LCL for lower control limit.)

The capability ratio C_r= 6σ/Total tolerance where the total tolerance is the USL − the LSL, or 0.411 − 0.397 = 0.014. Thus

$$C_r = 0.01032/0.014 = 0.737 \quad \text{or} \quad 73.7\%$$

Referring to Table 6.1, we can evaluate the process capability. C_r is less than 80%, the $\overline{X}$ chart is in control, and the specification nominal value, 0.4040, is within the control limits on the $\overline{X}$ chart, so the process capability is acceptable.

Attribute data

The capability of an attribute data process is the value of the center line or average. This value can be used only if the chart is in control. Suppose a process capability study is done with attribute data, and a p chart is used to plot the data. Suppose the chart is in control, and the value of the center line $\bar{p}$ is 5%. Then the capability of the process studied is 5%, and the process is capable of making 5% defective products. To determine if this is an acceptable value for the average percent defective requires a target or goal for comparison. If the target is 10%, then the process would be considered acceptable. If the target is 2%, then the process may be unacceptable.

Analysis.   Using the appropriate control chart, plot the subgroup values and determine the center line and control limits using the appropriate formulas. See Chaps. 7 and 8 of *Statistical Quality Control* by Grant and Leavenworth for examples of attribute control chart computations.

Evaluation.   Whether the process is acceptable, marginal, or unacceptable is determined by the relation of the center line (process average) to the target or goal. The criteria are defined as shown in Fig. 6.3. If the target or goal is above the UCL, then the process capability is acceptable. If the target or goal is between the UCL and the center line, the process is marginal. If the target or goal is below the center line, the process is unacceptable. If the process capability is marginal or unacceptable, determine and initiate corrective action. Use the corrective and preventive action matrix (Fig. 7.2) to define what actions are to be taken, who is to perform the actions, and when the actions are to be done. When the actions are completed, repeat the process capability study to determine if the actions were effective.

Example.   Suppose a process capability study is conducted on a printed-circuit-board wave-solder process. One of the important characteristics is the percentage of boards with "solder bridges." The target for the characteristic was set at 1%. A subgroup of 50 boards was selected every

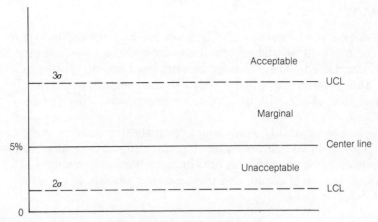

Figure 6.3 Process capability evaluation of attribute data.

2 hr from the wave-solder machine, and the number of boards with solder bridges was recorded. This was repeated until 25 subgroups were obtained.

When the study was completed, the data were plotted on the control chart for fraction defective (p chart), as shown in Fig. 6.4. The figure shows that the control chart is in control and that the process capability is 2.96%.

According to Fig. 6.3, the process can be determined as unacceptable since the target is 1%. The target is below the process average. The process is close to the target, but additional corrective action must be taken to reduce the process average to 1% or less.

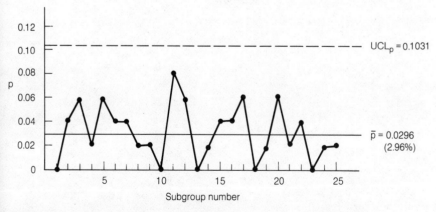

Figure 6.4 Control chart for a wave-solder process, showing solder bridges.

SUMMARY

The results of the process capability study are used primarily to determine the center lines and control limits for ongoing real-time process control charts. The IC study must be completed and acceptable before doing the process capability study. If any corrective actions are required, the study will be conducted again after the actions are completed.

The process capability study along with the IC study described in Chap. 5 are the two main steps for implementing SPC on any process. The team can now proceed with SPC implementation knowing that the inspection system is sound, and the process is capable of meeting the stated requirements.

Corrective and Preventive Action Matrix

The primary advantage that SPC provides is *real-time* feedback on the process. This feedback must be continuous and statistically founded, but it has no lasting value unless immediate corrective and preventive (CP) action is taken. It is this critical area of real-time feedback where most SPC implementation efforts fall short. When this situation exists, the manufacturing plants have a situation called *wallpaper*.

The real difference between success and failure is the time lapse between the occurrence of an out-of-control condition and the actions taken to bring the process back into control and to prevent the recurrence of the cause. An exceptionally effective *technique* to eliminate those delays is the CP action matrix, step 7 in the 12-step PQI process. This chapter defines CP action, develops a CP action matrix, and shows how to use it.

The CP action matrix helps operators to solve problems on their own. When a process goes out of control, the operator identifies the defect or defects and initiates the action indicated on the CP action matrix. It is usually posted next to the process control chart and events log.

The CP action matrix is a means for "closing the loop" in the application of SPC. It identifies the specific actions that must be taken to bring the process back in control. It also provides documented instructions that can be used to train new operators and engineers. The matrix is a listing of all known defects and conditions that can exist in the process being measured along with their respective CP action. (Each time a new defect or cause of defect is identified, the CP action matrix must be updated.) It is a troubleshooting guide that clearly outlines the steps to follow in order of likelihood of resolution. All of the problem solving and troubleshooting is done ahead of time, and solutions or actions are predetermined. So, when an out-of-control condition occurs, no time is wasted in deciding what to do first. Figure 7.1 illustrates the ongoing SPC loop.

The process control chart tells those in direct control of the operation when to take action: the CP action matrix tells them what action to take to bring the *process* back to a state of statistical control and what to do with the defective or suspect *product*. The CP action matrix actually replaces the floor activity of the material review board (MRB).

CP Action

Since the words *corrective* and *preventive* can be interpreted differently depending on their focus, the following definitions are used in this chapter.

Corrective action

Corrective action is that action taken to address the *defect* in the product or incoming parts, materials, and so on; to purge suspected products through the last acceptable subgroup (i.e., identify suspected material for the defects of issue that caused the process to go out of control) and subsequently sort the product for the defects; and to rework the defect or replace parts on the product to make the product conform to specifications.

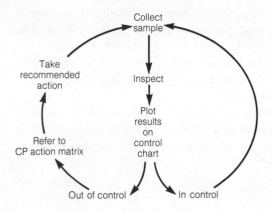

Figure 7.1 Ongoing SPC loop.

For example, when a process goes out of control, it contains one or more defects. It is imperative to have clear direction about what to do with the product produced since the last acceptable subgroup. This product is now suspect, and corrective action needs to be identified for the defects found in the sample and subsequent product up to the last acceptable subgroup. For an out-of-control point (dimension) for a grinding machine, the corrective action could be to purge for defects for the specific dimension through the last acceptable subgroup, purge those parts for the defects, and regrind the defective parts.

Preventive action

Preventive action is that action taken to remove the *cause* of the defect that produced the out-of-control process or preceding processes and to prevent the cause from recurring. The main objective of this action is to bring the process permanently back in control.

For example, suppose a grinding control chart for a grinding machine goes out of control. The preventive action could be to adjust the grinding machines index wheel to compensate for the wear.

Contingent action

Another action, similar to corrective action, is contingent action. Although we define them differently, we handle them together as corrective action for operational simplicity. *Contingent action* is action that limits the impact of defects or that temporarily stops the input of defect sources from previous processes. However, it does not address the root cause of the defect. Examples are the screening of incoming material or parts from previous process, stores, or suppliers.

In the case of the grinding machine, one could take contingent action on screening for excessive weld flash from a previous process should that be found to be the cause of the defects. Then preventive action would be to eliminate the cause of defects for the weld excess at the weld process.

CP Action Matrix Development

The CP action matrix is primarily used to bring a process back in control. It allows almost anyone in the process to solve problems. The documented defects and their respective CP actions offer the operator a troubleshooting guide that has been developed and proven by manufacturing and quality engineers. A process goes out of control because some change in the process has occurred. The people involved in developing a CP action matrix should be those who have the most experience with the changes and know how to alleviate the undesirable condition.

The six major sections of the CP action matrix in Fig. 7.2 are defect or condition, probable cause, defect type, station responsible, corrective action, and preventive action. To prepare a CP action matrix using this format, follow these steps.

Defect or condition.   Begin by identifying all potential defects or conditions (for an $\overline{X}$ and R chart) that you would expect to find at the inspection point being addressed. For a mature operation most defects have probably already been experienced. If there are many probable defects, such as for an attribute chart, select the most critical or most frequent defects. Pareto's 80/20 rule may be applicable in this case—that is, 20% of the defects cause 80% of the problems.

Probable cause.   Establish the probable cause for each defect or condition identified. The purpose of this section is to further clarify the problem and help to identify preventive action. The likelihood of having more than one probable cause per defect or condition is high. When this happens, list the probable causes in order of priority, with the most likely cause first. The entire team preparing the matrix should agree on probable causes and their order of priority. If this cannot be done, it usually means that no one really knows what creates the undesirable condition and further analysis must be conducted (see techniques in Chap. 4), independently of the development of the matrix, to determine the cause.

Defect type.   Knowing the type of defect or condition being addressed helps establish accountability for preventing the undesirable condition. The four types of defects are workmanship, product design, process, and component (or materials). (See Table 7.1.) If defects or errors are not assignable, the manufacturing engineers receive defects in a category called *unknown*. The defect remains assigned to the manufacturing engineer until he or she assigns it a type.

Table 7.2 gives some guidelines for CP actions.

Workmanship defects should be addressed by a separate corporate quality policy referred to in the CP action matrix. The policy should help operators to improve their performance and still maintain a progressive step process.

1. Initial out-of-control condition

Action required.   The supervisor informs the responsible operator or inspector of the defect. It is best to show the defect to the individual

Corrective and Preventive Action Matrix

Inspection station: _____
Product: _____
Inspection instruction: _____
Date: _____ Revision: _____

Prepared by: _____
Date effective: _____
Approved by: _____

Page _____ of _____
Revised by: _____
Date effective: _____
Approved by: _____

Defect or condition	Probable cause	Defect type (W, D, P, C)*	Station responsible	Corrective action† (addresses defect)	Preventive action (addresses cause)		
					Operator	Inspector	Other

* Workmanship, product design, process, component.
† Before any action is taken, defect must be positively identified.

Figure 7.2 CP action matrix.

123

TABLE 7.1   Defect Types, for use with CP Action Matrix

Defect type	Description	Station responsible
Workmanship	Defects or errors caused by intentionally or unintentionally not following the prescribed method or process	Production
Product design	Defects caused by deficiencies in the product design or specifications (e.g., errors that are caused by a tolerance buildup)	Design engineering
Process	Defects resulting from a work element due to improper methods, tooling, or equipment	Manufacturing or process engineering
Component	Defects resulting from defective parts, components, or raw materials that are used to produce the product; could be internal or external suppliers	Quality engineering

and make sure he or she knows the acceptance criteria. No disciplinary action is taken.

Comment. This action will solve most workmanship defects.

2. Second occurrence (the frequency must be determined by the nature and volume of the process)

Action required. Conduct a process audit on the process and on the operator or inspector. A trained quality engineer or inspection supervisor performs a diagnostic process audit on the production operator. If an inspector is involved, a manufacturing engineer and production supervisor would conduct the audit.

The purpose of the audit (refer to Chap. 4) is to determine (1) if the documentation, tools, or other process variables are acceptable, and (2) if the operator or inspector is complying to the documentation. Frequently, the operator or inspector can precisely identify the cause of the problem. Normally the causes are management's responsibility. If the audit is unacceptable, then the appropriate preventive action must be taken, and the process subsequently reaudited to determine the effectiveness of that action. No disciplinary action is taken.

The following table lists some preventive actions:

Deficiency	Action
Documentation	Rewrite more detailed and clear instructions.
Process	Provide effective tools, gages, etc.
Training	Increase the operator's knowledge of the process and acceptance criteria, and test for competency by an inspection capability study.

If the audit is acceptable and the operator or inspector was complying with the documentation, the operator is certified as knowing the process.

Comment. The process audit will identify a large percentage of the causes. The causes are normally the responsibility of management, not the operator.

3. Third occurrence (the frequency must be determined by the nature and volume of the process)

Action required. A verbal warning is given (first step of disciplinary action). The supervisor will verify the defects and give the respon-

TABLE 7.2   Guidelines for CP Action

Defect type	Corrective action	Preventive action
Workmanship	Purge Rework or repair Reinspection	Operator awareness Process audit Compliance to corporate workmanship quality policy
Product design	Replace Rework Stress screening with appropriate stimuli Purge Reinspection	Engineering change request Engineering change order implemented
Process	Rework Repair Purge Reinspection	Adjust equipment and variables Repair tooling, equipment, etc. Replace tooling, equipment, etc.
Component	Rework Repair Screen incoming Purge	Address cause at suppliers

sible operator or inspector a verbal warning for quality. Prerequisites would be successful closures on the operator awareness and process audit steps.

Comment. Seldom is this action needed. However, it is suggested that a corporate workmanship quality policy be written, even though it may never be used.

4. Fourth occurrence (the frequency must be determined by the nature and volume of the process)

Action required. A written warning is given (second step of disciplinary action). The supervisor will verify the defects and give the responsible operator or inspector a written warning. Prerequisites would be successful closures on the operator awareness and process audit steps and a verbal warning.

Comment. Rarely is this done. Its value is that it does exist just in case it is needed.

5. Fifth occurrence (the frequency must be determined by the nature and volume of the process)

Action required. The operator is suspended (third step of disciplinary action). The supervisor will verify the defects and will suspend the operator or inspector. Prerequisites would be successful completion of the awareness step, process audit, and verbal and written warnings.

Comment. Very rarely does this occur.

6. Sixth occurrence (the frequency must be determined by the nature and volume of the process)

Action required. The operator is fired (fourth step of disciplinary action). The supervisor will verify the defects and will fire the responsible operator or inspector. Prerequisites would be successful completion of awareness, process audit, verbal warning, written warning, and suspension.

Comment. I have never seen this happen.

In summary, workmanship defects can be resolved by addressing the foregoing six steps. The first two steps will yield acceptable quality 98% of the time.

Station responsible. Identify the responsible station where the defect or condition originates. This is the station where preventive action will be taken for the specific defect or condition when the process goes out of control.

Corrective action. Establish the corrective action to make the product conform to specification. These actions should include purging, i.e., identifying the defective product and reworking it as needed. The team must decide what actions are economically most appropriate and list them in order of preference or consensus. Since the defects have probably already been seen before, it is also likely that some corrective action exists. There may be even more corrective actions or options than necessary. Then the best action must be chosen. This can also be accomplished by consensus. If a consensus cannot be reached, the manufacturing engineer should prepare a cost analysis and feasibility study of the alternatives. Sometimes it is more economical to scrap a product than to rework it.

Corrective action addresses the defect in the product or incoming parts. Regardless of the probable cause, the corrective actions will always be the same for a particular defect or condition. Examples of corrective actions are remove the defective component and replace it, grind or remove excessive material from the component, sand and repaint the component, and screen incoming parts or materials for defects.

Preventive action. Preventive action is established to remove the cause of the defects leading to an out-of-control process or previous processes and to bring the process back into a state of statistical control. Establish at least one preventive action for each probable cause identified. If more than one action is identified, list them in order of effectiveness, from left to right. In determining effectiveness, consider the time and the cost to implement the action. As with corrective action select the best action currently available. If a consensus cannot be reached, then assign a member of the team to analyze the alternatives or develop new ones. Preventive actions include adjust tooling, reset cutting bit, adjust machine, repair equipment, or retrain operator.

Often the same CP actions will be specified for different defects, conditions, or probable causes. Hence coding of CP actions is recommended. For example, use numbers for corrective action and letters for preventive action. The codes and definitions should be on a separate sheet and attached to the matrix.

Using the Matrix

When faced with an out-of-control condition, whether a point outside the process control limits, a shift, or a trend, the team must take action to eliminate the cause and make the product conform to specifications. The first action is a review of the control chart to determine what condition or defect caused the out-of-control situation. The team next reviews the CP action matrix and locates the defect or condition by tracing the matrix horizontally to determine the appropriate actions and where they should be taken. Preventive actions are applied first; corrective actions next. The actions identified for the first probable cause listed are chosen. For preventive action, if the cause is known and is other than the first one listed, the team starts with the known cause and takes the action listed. It records the defect and actions taken on the process control chart in the proper space.

Corrective action must be taken as soon as possible, before the product is delivered to its internal customer, but preventive action must be taken *immediately*. Preventive action keeps further defective products from being produced. This action is performed at the responsible station as indicated on the matrix. The team takes the first preventive action listed on the matrix for the particular probable cause and verifies that it has removed the cause and that the process is again producing acceptable product (is in control). If the action is not effective or has not removed the cause, the team takes the next action listed on the matrix for that cause. If all actions associated with the first probable cause have been exhausted and the problem continues, the team proceeds to the next probable cause and follows the same steps. If a second or subsequent probable cause has not been identified, then a condition exists for which the cause is unknown. This may sound familiar. It is how a "problem" was defined in Chap. 4. When the process is out of control and the cause is not known, the options are commonly limited to stopping the process or inspecting the product 100% until cause and preventive action are identified. To find the cause, the team applies the most appropriate technique from Chap. 4. Once the cause and preventive action have been identified the CP action matrix must be updated to reflect the new information.

SUMMARY

The CP action matrix is a powerful auxiliary SPC tool. It clearly defines the actions that must be taken to address any defective product produced, and the actions that must be taken immediately to prevent recurrence of that problem in the future. It further identifies *who* is responsible for taking the action. It also completely supports the real-time philosophy of SPC, since all the problem analysis and solutions are identified ahead of time instead of waiting until a problem condition appears. It empowers the operators to solve the problem with minimum assistance from the engineering staff and provides consistency in solving problems over time.

Process Control Procedure*

Effective SPC goes far beyond just monitoring process control charts. The "signals" given by the charts must be interpreted properly, and the appropriate actions must be taken by people who know how to interpret them and know what their responsibilities are. The modus operandi for the team to ensure that results are achieved is a *process control procedure,* step 8 in the PQI process.

This chapter discusses the purpose of step 8—to provide quality history, control chart rationale, operating instructions, and system documentation for installing and sustaining SPC. It defines the requirements and responsibilities for the three phases of effective SPC: (1) initial requirements (implementation), (2) ongoing requirements (execution), and (3) review and analysis (sustainment).

When writing the process control procedure, the team must make sure that it contains the requirements for

- The history of the process, the background on the defects, and so on
- Selecting the type of chart and the subgroup size and frequency
- Determining if the process is in a state of SPC
- Identifying out-of-control situations
- Identifying when to search for the cause of defects and when to take CP action

---

*Ignacio Munoz participated in preparing this chapter.

The procedure must also identify the tools and methods for sustaining the process within SPC. We have already discussed most of these tools and methods. The procedure must also define and assign responsibility and accountability for the actions and elements of the SPC process, such as selecting and implementing control charts and establishing control limits, reviewing and analyzing the charts, and developing guidelines and assigning the authority for shutting down a process.

Many other responsibilities must be included, but the responsible positions will vary from company to company. The emphasis of the procedure, however, must clearly be management action: specify the responsible *people*, their *duties*, and the *methods* they will use.

Initial Requirements

The initial requirements for SPC involve (1) selecting control charts and establishing limits (see Chap. 9), (2) CP action matrix, (3) events log, and (4) posting control charts.

Selecting control charts and establishing limits

Selecting the control chart involves determining the characteristic to be measured, the type of chart, the rationale for subgroup selection, the subgroup size, the subgroup frequency, and the ongoing center line and control limits. Data for the initial limits are usually obtained from the process capability study conducted by the manufacturing engineer. If the process is in control and capable of producing at the nominal or target value, the center line and control limits measured are the initial values to use for the ongoing control chart. The process capability study is the culmination of activities beginning with the flow diagram that identifies the characteristics and the part of the process to be controlled.

When it is not practical or economical to do a process capability study, actual data from the process may be used without controlling the data collection according to the guidelines described for a process capability study. If the process is found to be in control after collecting these data, those center line and control limit values may be used for the initial ongoing control chart. The risk in using this alternative and bypassing the guidelines is that any abnormal variation becomes part of the natural variation of the process. The quality engineer in this case has the responsibility to evaluate the results and select the appropriate chart to be used.

CP action matrix

The CP action matrix developed in step 7 lists the history of problems encountered at a particular operation, including actions taken to correct and prevent their recurrence. A CP action matrix must be posted for each control chart application. The team should develop the matrix as a coordinated effort, but the manufacturing engineer is responsible for completing and posting it.

Events log

An events log is required for all operations under SPC. The log consists of entries from anyone associated with the process that has information on anything new, different, or changed. Preparation and posting of the events log is the responsibility of the manufacturing engineer.

Posting control charts

Setting up and posting control charts is the responsibility of the quality engineer. All process control charts should be posted at or near the operation being monitored. Special display boards that are designed for easy chart removal, data posting, and chart analysis are helpful. Additional space must be provided for the CP action matrix and events log. Control charts should be on paper to provide a permanent record, and the previous charts should be attached beneath the current chart.

Ongoing Requirements

The elements to consider for ongoing requirements are (1) posting control charts, (2) checking for out-of-control conditions, both in the favorable as well as unfavorable directions, and (3) responding to out-of-control conditions.

Posting control charts

The control charts should be posted near the process they are measuring. The charts should be clearly visible and easily accessible.

After the charts are initially posted by the quality engineer, the production operator or inspector must maintain them. The operator or inspector obtains and inspects samples, records results, and plots data on control charts as required (see Fig. 8.1). Completed charts are analyzed and recorded by the quality engineer. A new chart with control limits and other pertinent information is provided by an assigned staff person.

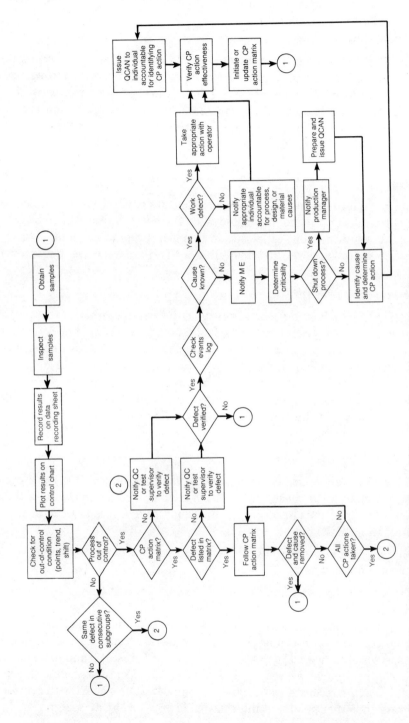

Figure 8.1 SPC process flow diagram. CP stands for corrective and preventive, ME for mechanical engineering, QC for quality control, and QCAN for quality control action notice.

Checking for out-of-control conditions

An out-of-control condition exists if (1) one or more points are outside either control limit; or there are (2) seven consecutive points above or below the center line; or there are (3) seven or more points in the same upward or downward direction (trend). Variations of tests (2) and (3) may be used, but because they are based on the laws of probability, any variations in the tests will increase or decrease the probability of detecting abnormal conditions in the process. For example, the probability of having seven points in a row above or below the center line is 0.008.

Everyone associated with the process—quality engineer, production operator, inspector, and production supervisors—is responsible for checking the charts for out-of-control conditions. When applicable, it is important to identify the cause of out-of-control points on the favorable control limit so one can repeat the performance.

Responding to out-of-control conditions

When a control chart shows that an out-of-control condition exists, the operator, inspector, and their supervisors must immediately follow the instructions in the CP action matrix for the particular problem. If the matrix is correct and up to date, personnel should resolve the problem by following the directions on the matrix. If the defect continues after all listed actions are completed, a quality control action notice (QCAN) should be issued by the quality engineer. The QCAN is issued to request CP action, to determine if the process should be stopped, and to advise management of the process condition. The process should be stopped when the criticality of the defect will have major impact on safety, customer satisfaction, or rework costs. The QCAN will be covered in greater detail later in this chapter.

The production operator or supervisor must indicate all out-of-control points on the chart by placing a ◯ near the out-of-control point and numbering the circles as shown on Fig. 8.2. The cause for each out-of-control point and the corrective action taken must be listed on the control chart for each ◯. The defect, its cause, and the corresponding CP action should already be listed on the CP action matrix. If not, the action taken to remove the cause of the defect must be added to the matrix to help in identifying future causes of defects.

Review and Analysis

All SPC charts must be reviewed periodically to ensure that they are up-to-date. Production and quality supervisors must annotate the charts

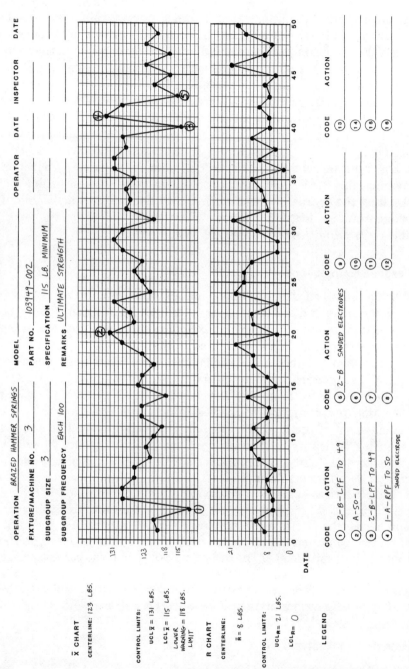

Figure 8.2 Process control chart.

at least twice a day. Manufacturing and quality engineers must review and annotate the charts at least once a day.

The team must establish how often data collection forms and control charts should be submitted, and who should review the data for the purpose of revising the limits. Although the frequency of review will vary, depending on the maturity and quality history of the process, the following guidelines are useful: (1) Attribute control chart center-line values should only be changed downward. The center-line values should not be increased to reflect a deteriorating process. In this case a recovery plan should be developed. (2) The range chart for variable control charts should be reviewed closely. If the average range has increased, the process needs correction. If the average range has decreased, the limits should be changed. The quality engineer will calculate new limits as required and publish a matrix of current and revised limits for those supervisors and plant managers affected by the changes. See Fig. 8.3.

CP Action

Processes whose subgroups vary around the center line when plotted and remain within the control limits are said to be within SPC. Any variation is due to chance causes. When any point is outside the control limits or there is evidence of a trend, the process is considered out of control. (See Fig. 8.4.)

When writing the process control procedure (see Fig. 8.5), the team should include the following procedure: When a point goes out of control and a CP action matrix exists, the area supervisor for the process will take action according to the most likely cause listed on the CP action matrix. The inspector and inspection supervisor will verify that the problem has been corrected, by auditing subsequent units. If the problem has been corrected, the normal process continues. If the problem has not been corrected, the actions listed on the CP action matrix must be implemented until all possible actions have been taken.

When a defect is not listed on a CP action matrix, the area supervisor must notify the quality control supervisor to have the defect verified. If the QC supervisor is not available, the area supervisor should notify the QC manager immediately. The QC supervisor (or manager) will verify the defect and determine if the reject is valid. Valid rejects will require that the area supervisor immediately determine and remove the cause. If the cause is workmanship related, the supervisor must take the appropriate action to correct the problem and to verify that the defect is eliminated. If the cause is not workmanship, the supervisor must notify the accountable manufacturing engineer, who must

	Current			Actual			New		
Station or operator number	Center line	UCL	LCL	Center line	UCL	LCL	Center line	UCL	LCL

Quality engineer: _____ Product line: _____

Date: _____

Approved by: _____
QE manager

Figure 8.3 Process control procedure support data.

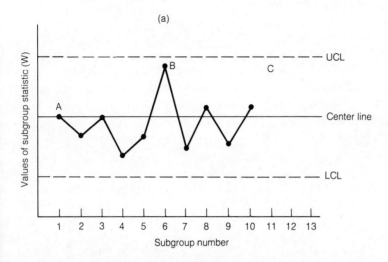

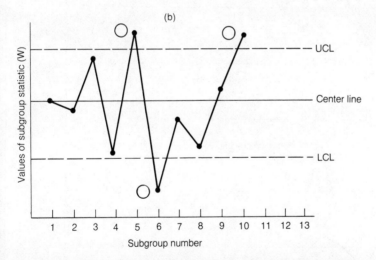

Figure 8.4   (*a*) Control chart showing in-control process. Points form a natural pattern. A: Most points near center line. B: A few points near control limits. C: No points beyond control limits. (*b*)–(*k*) are control charts showing out-of-control conditions. The causes are as follows. (*b*) One or more points outside control limits. (*c*) Trend. (*d*) 7 points in a row shift above center line. (*e*) 7 points in a row shift below center line. (*f*) 10 out of 11 points on same side of center line. (*g*) 12 out of 14 points on same side of center line. (*h*) More than 7 points on one side of center line. (*i*) 10 out of 11 points, and 7 points in a row, above center line. (*j*) Trend: 7 points in one direction without change in direction. (*k*) Trend: 8 or more points in one direction.

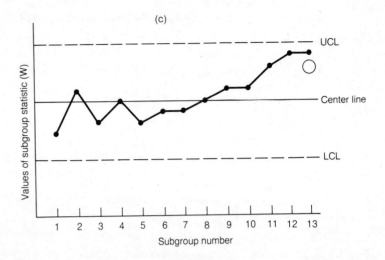

(c)

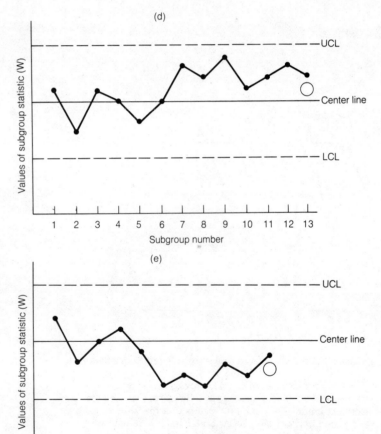

(d)

(e)

Figure 8.4 (*Continued*)

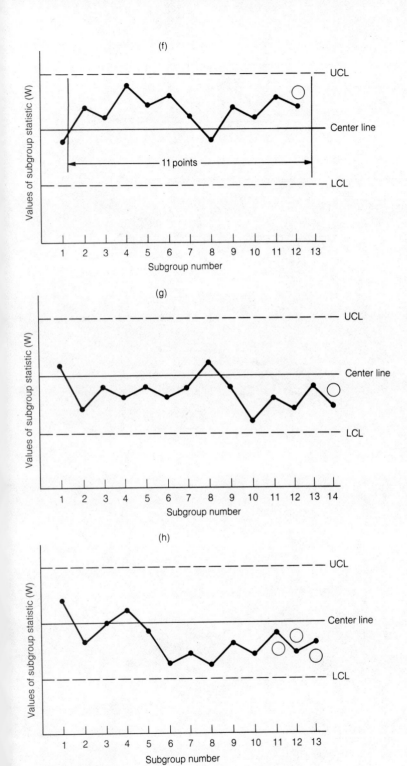

Figure 8.4 (*Continued*)

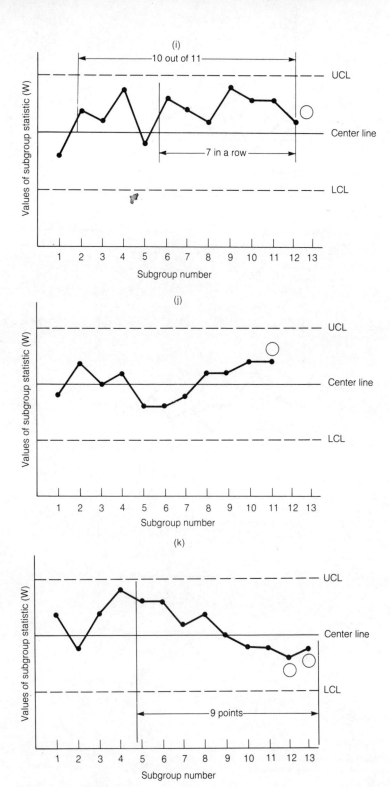

Figure 8.4 (*Continued*)

Date: Revision _____   Control No. _____
Subject: Process control procedure

1.0. Purpose. To establish the system for introducing and maintaining statistical process control (SPC), and to communicate instructions and requirements for identifying out-of-control situations.
  1.1. To provide rationale for the selection of the control chart, subgroups, and subgroup frequency.
  1.2. To determine if the measured production process is in a state of SPC.
  1.3. To identify when to search for the cause of defects and when to take corrective and preventive action.
  1.4. To maintain the process within statistical control.
2.0. Scope. This procedure applies to the manufacture of (specify product) which is tracked by and controlled with SPC methods.
3.0. Organizational units affected.
  3.1. Production.
  3.2. Inspection (quality control).
  3.3. Manufacturing engineering.
  3.4. Quality engineering.
  3.5. Quality assurance.
  3.6. Test engineering.
4.0. Definitions.
  4.1. Process control chart. A graph which plots the statistic $\bar{X}$, R, u, p, or c, calculated from subgroups (samples) collected periodically over time. The process control chart is characterized by a center line (process average) and upper and lower control limits. A process is judged in control if all points fall within the control limits, which are located three standard deviations away from the process average. A process is judged to be out of control if any point falls outside the control limits or there is an indication of a trend or shift.
  4.2. State of statistical control. An expression which describes a process which exhibits natural variation and reflects a constant cause system. Also known as a process which is in control.
  4.3. Corrective action. Actions taken to assure that all suspect material is identified, verified, and corrected; that is, purge, sort, rework, reinspect, use as is.
  4.4. Preventive action. Actions taken to address the cause of out-of-control conditions and to bring the process back to a state of statistical control.
  4.5. Quality control action notice (QCAN). A document issued to initiate corrective action and/or preventive action on a process that is out of control. It may be issued to shut down or correct the process. (See Section 10.0.)
  4.6. Corrective and preventive (CP) action matrix. A document which lists the defects expected to be seen at an inspection and test station and the respective CP actions to be taken if the process goes out of control.
  4.7. Process capability study. A technique used to determine the capability of the natural variation of the process and its limits for ongoing process control.
  4.8. Purge. Actions taken to identify suspect units, examine the units for specific defects and their causes, and segregate units with defects from regular production.
5.0. History.
  5.1. A statement of current and the past three months' quality performance should be provided. This should be quantified and be expressed in percent defective, defects per unit or preferably defects per 1000 units, or defects per million opportunities. The selection should be the most applicable for the quality indicator.
  5.2. A list of all defects produced by the process should be provided.
  5.3. The defects should be referenced to a quality document which contains criteria for acceptance.
6.0. Rationale.
  6.1. Selection of the type of control chart. A statement is required which identifies the type of control chart selected and the reasons for and advantages of its selection.

Figure 8.5 Process control procedure.

6.2. Selection of rationale subgroups. A statement is required which identifies how the subgroups were selected (i.e., progressively, randomly) and the reasons for their selection. The size of the subgroup and reasons that the size was selected should be stated.

6.3. Frequency of subgroups. A statement of what the original frequency should be and the strategy for reducing the frequency are required. The reasons should support the original selections and strategy.

6.4. Revisions to rationale. A change of control chart type and revisions to subgroup rationale, subgroup size, or frequency of subgroups should be recorded and explained.

7.0. Requirements and responsibilities.

    7.1. Initial requirements for establishing current and future SPC.

        7.1.1. Initiate events log as described in the problem analysis procedure. Responsibility: Manufacturing engineer.

        7.1.2. Select appropriate control chart ($\bar{X}$, R, p, c, u, np) and subgroup size. Responsibility: Quality engineer.

        7.1.3. Establish ongoing center line and control limits as described in Section 8.0. Responsibility: Quality engineer.

        7.1.4. Prepare a CP action matrix. Responsibility: Manufacturing engineer.

        7.1.5. Set up and post initial process control charts. Responsibility: Area supervisor.

        7.1.6. Provide a place to which control charts can be attached. Responsibility: Manufacturing engineer.

    7.2. Ongoing requirements (data collection and use).

        7.2.1. Update and post control charts at appropriate stations. Responsibility: Inspector, tester, and/or operator.

        7.2.2. Obtain and inspect samples. Record results on data collection forms and plot data on control charts as required. Responsibility: Inspector, tester, and/or operator.

        7.2.3. Check for out-of-control conditions. Notify inspection and test supervisor.

            7.2.3.1. Out-of-control conditions can be detected through one or more of the tests shown in Fig. 8.4 with normal control limits. Responsibility: Inspector, tester, operator.

            7.2.3.2. A point outside the control limits with modified control limits indicates an out-of-control condition. When a pattern of out-of-control points exists, revert to normal control limits.

            7.2.3.3. Continuing defects are an indication that previous preventive action was not effective; see Section 9.3. Responsibility: Inspection supervisor, assembly supervisor, test supervisor.

            7.2.3.4. Special situation. When the process is in control, improvement is desired, and none is being observed, and when two identical defects are observed in the same subgroup, three identical defects are observed in the same day, or four identical defects are observed in the same week, action on attribute control charts should be initiated. Further improvement of the process can be undertaken even with other frequencies of defects. Common sense should prevail.

        7.2.4. Initiate actions for out-of-control conditions as described in Section 9.0. Responsibility: Inspection supervisor, test supervisor, and/or production supervisor.

        7.2.5. Record actions taken for out-of-control points in the legend of the control chart. Responsibility: Supervisor, inspector, tester, and/or operator.

    7.3. Ongoing review and analysis of process control charts.

        7.3.1. Review data on control charts and initial.

            7.3.1.1. Supervisors are to review and initial charts a minimum of two times a day. Responsibility: Inspection supervisor, test supervisor, assembly supervisor.

            7.3.1.2. Engineers are to review and initial charts a minimum of once a day. Responsibility: Manufacturing engineer, quality engineer.

        7.3.2. Submit completed data collection forms and control charts to quality engineering for review and analysis. Responsibility: Inspection supervisor, test supervisor, assembly supervisor.

Figure 8.5 *(Continued)*

7.3.3. Review completed charts and analyze as described in Section 8.2. Responsibility: Quality Engineer.
8.0. Establishing control limits.
  8.1. Initial control limits.
    8.1.1. Preferred method.
      8.1.1.1. Data for the initial limits are obtained by conducting a process capability study. Responsibility: Manufacturing engineer, test engineer, quality engineer.
      8.1.1.2. The process must be in control and capable. The center line and control limits found in the process capability study are then adopted. These values or modified limits, if appropriate, are the initial values used for the ongoing control chart. Responsibility: Manufacturing engineer, quality engineer, and test engineer.
    8.1.2. Alternate method. Data for initial control limits may also be established by obtaining samples from the ongoing process for a minimum of 25 subgroups. If the process is in control, the center-line value and control limits may be used for the initial ongoing control chart. If the process is out of control, correct the process and redo 25 subgroups of data. An in-control process must be achieved before establishing limits for an ongoing chart. Responsibility: Quality engineer or manufacturing engineer.
  8.2. Ongoing control limit revisions. The completed charts are reviewed a minimum of once a month, preferably once a week, to determine if the center-line and control limit values have changed. Responsibility: Quality engineer.
    8.2.1. Attribute control chart center-line values will only be modified downward. The center-line values (p, c) will not be increased to reflect a deteriorating process. Appropriate CP action should be taken to return the process to control when the chart indicates the process has gone out of control or shifted. Responsibility: Manufacturing engineer, test engineer, quality engineer, and/or production supervisor.
    8.2.2. The range for variable control charts should be reviewed closely. If R has increased, the process needs correction. If R has decreased, the limits should be changed. Consider use of modified limits if the estimate of process spread $6 \ (\bar{R}/d_2)$ is 60% or less of total tolerance. Responsibility: Quality engineer.
    8.2.3. Distribute a matrix of current, calculated, and new limits to plant management and supervision. Responsibility: Quality engineer.
9.0. CP action.
  9.1. CP action matrix exists: defect is listed on the matrix.
    9.1.1. Supervisor or designee takes action according to the CP action matrix. Responsibility: Test supervisor, inspection supervisor (if needed), assembly supervisor.
    9.1.2. Supervisor or designee verifies that the problem has been corrected by auditing subsequent units.
      9.1.2.1. If a problem has been corrected, proceed with normal process.
      9.1.2.2. If a problem has not been corrected, repeat steps 9.1.1 and 9.1.2 until all actions on the CP action matrix have been taken.
      9.1.2.3. If the problem persists after taking all actions on the CP action matrix, proceed with step 9.3.1. Responsibility: Inspection supervisor, test supervisor.
  9.2. CP action matrix does not exist or defect is not listed on any existing matrix.
    9.2.1. Have the quality engineer verify the defect. If he or she is not available, notify the appropriate manager immediately. Responsibility: Inspection supervisor, test supervisor, and/or assembly supervisor.
    9.2.2. Verify the defect and determine if the rejection is valid. Responsibility: Quality engineer.
      9.2.2.1. If the rejection is not valid, notify the appropriate supervisor and proceed with the normal process (remove data from the chart). Responsibility: Quality engineer.
      9.2.2.2. If the rejection is valid, have the appropriate supervisor determine cause. Responsibility: Quality engineer.
    9.2.3. Determine if cause of defect is known. Responsibility: Inspection supervisor, test supervisor, assembly supervisor.

Figure 8.5   *(Continued)*

144   Chapter 8

9.2.3.1. If cause is due to workmanship, take appropriate action to correct the problem and proceed with step 9.2.6. Responsibility: Assembly supervisor, inspection supervisor, test supervisor.

9.2.3.2. If the cause is known and it is not due to workmanship, notify the responsible individual (proceed with step 9.2.5). Responsibility: Assembly supervisor.

Cause	Responsibility
Process	Manufacturing engineer
Component	Quality engineer
Design	Design engineer

9.2.3.3. If the cause is unknown, notify the manufacturing engineer immediately. If he or she is unavailable, notify manufacturing engineering management. Responsibility: Assembly supervisor.

9.2.4. Determine criticality of the defect and recommend continuation or shutdown of the process to production management. Responsibility: Quality engineer, manufacturing engineer.

9.2.4.1. When required, shut down the operation. Responsibility: Production manager.

9.2.4.2. Issue a QCAN to the responsible individual (see Section 10.0). Responsibility: Quality engineer.

9.2.5. Identify cause of defect, determine CP action, and implement CP action. Responsibility: Manufacturing engineer.

9.2.6. Workmanship defects. (This section may be included on a separate policy statement and not on the copy on the production floor.) The following steps should be taken.

9.2.6.1. Make operator or inspector aware of defect. Note his or her name or employee number.

9.2.6.2. If defects continue, conduct a process audit and correct the process, material, or operator, as applicable.

9.2.6.3. If defects continue and process audit has been conducted and is determined to be acceptable, then give the operator a verbal warning.

9.2.6.4. If defects continue and operator has had a verbal warning, then give the operator a written warning.

9.2.6.5. If defects continue and operator has had a written warning, then suspend the operator.

9.2.6.6. If defects continue and operator has been suspended, then fire the operator.

9.2.7. Verify effectiveness of preventive action.

9.2.8. Initiate or update CP action matrix. Responsibility: Manufacturing engineer.

9.3. CP action matrix exists: actions listed partially solve the problem; CP action matrix does not solve the problem; two points out of control within last eight subgroups; same defect on three consecutive subgroups which are in control.

9.3.1. Have the quality engineer and manufacturing engineer verify the defect. If they are unavailable, notify the appropriate manager immediately. Responsibility: Production supervisor.

9.3.2. Verify the defect and determine if rejection is valid. Responsibility: Quality engineer, manufacturing engineer.

9.3.2.1. If the rejection is not valid, notify the assembly supervisor and proceed with the normal process. Make the reject acceptable on the control chart by crossing out the date and initialing and writing in the correct data. Responsibility: Quality engineer, manufacturing engineer.

9.3.3. If defect is verified, determine its criticality and recommend continuation or shutdown of the process to production management. Responsibility: Quality engineer, manufacturing engineer.

9.3.3.1. When required, shut down the operation. Responsibility: Production manager.

Figure 8.5 (*Continued*)

9.3.3.2. Prepare a QCAN and review problem with Production supervisor. Responsibility: Quality engineer.

9.3.4. Determine if defect cause is known. Responsibility: Quality engineer, manufacturing engineer.

9.3.4.1. If defect cause is known, issue QCAN to the responsible individual and verify effectiveness of preventive action. Responsibility: Quality engineer.

9.3.4.2. If defect cause is unknown, issue QCAN to manufacturing engineering for identification of cause. Responsibility: Quality engineer.

9.3.5. Identify cause and determine CP action (return to step 9.2.7). Responsibility: Manufacturing engineer.

10.0. Quality control action notice (QCAN).

10.1. Prepare and issue a QCAN to request CP action.

10.1.1. When a defect with an unknown cause exists.

10.1.2. When a problem persists after taking CP action (see Section 9.3 for criteria).

10.2. Shut down the process when the criticality of the defect will have a major impact, as described below. Responsibility: Production manager.

10.2.1. Safety. If defect will jeopardize the safety of those working on, or those who will be working on, the product.

10.2.2. Rework cost. If defect will be costly to repair in terms of both disassembly/assembly time and scrap.

10.2.3. Defect interaction. If defect is suspected of leading to a chain reaction of failures.

10.3. Distribute copies of QCAN.

10.3.1. Production manager.

10.3.2. Engineering manager.

10.3.3. Quality manager (QCAN file).

10.3.4. Test engineering.

10.4. Maintain shutdown status until CP action is taken.

10.5. Take CP action.

10.6. Purge line of suspected nonconforming material. Sort off line according to established procedure.

10.7. Perform a first-article inspection. Inspect the equivalent of one subgroup. If in-control,

10.8. Resume operation.

10.9. Follow up to assure that CP action is effective.

11.0. Audit for effectiveness.

11.1. Review completed QCANs for compliance and effectiveness of CP action.

11.2. Review process control charts according to process audit procedure (step 12 of 12-step program).

Figure 8.5 (*Continued*)

determine and implement corrective action. If the cause is unknown, the manufacturing engineer or manager must be notified to investigate and remove the cause.

The area quality engineer and the manufacturing engineer will determine the criticality of the defect and recommend continuation or shutdown of the process. If shutdown is required, they will issue a QCAN and notify the area production and QC managers. The process then cannot be restarted until the cause of the defect is eliminated.

Solutions listed on the CP action matrix that only partially solve the problem require the same action as for those not listed.

Quality Control Action Notice

To _____   QCAN no. _____
Dept. _____   Date _____
                            By _____
                            Operation _____
                            Machine no. _____
                            Shift _____

Shut down process?   Reason(s)

Yes _____   _____ 1 or more points beyond either control limit
No _____   _____ 7 points in a row above the process average
                         _____ 7 points in a row below the process average
                         _____ 7 points in an upward trend
                         _____ 7 points in a downward trend

Corrective action

Description of defects out of control _____

Purge required? No Yes   If yes, through previous accepted subgroup or other?
Completed by _____   Dept. _____   Date _____

Preventive action

Completed by _____   Dept. _____   Date _____

                                            Target date _____

Followup

Corrective action	Preventive action	Followup
Accepted	Accepted	Date _____
Rejected	Rejected	QE _____
QE _____	QE _____	New QCAN no. _____

Figure 8.6   Quality control action notice (QCAN).

Quality control action notice (QCAN)

A QCAN (Fig. 8.6) is a document issued by the quality engineer to initiate CP action on an out-of-control process. It may be issued to shut down or correct the process whenever

- A defect with an unknown cause exists
- A problem persists because the CP action was ineffective
- The criticality of the defect will have a major impact on safety, rework costs, or customer satisfaction, or if this defect will cause the failure of a related part

Copies of the QCAN should be distributed to ME, QE, QC, production managers, and area supervisors.

The shutdown will be maintained until corrective action has been taken to purge the defective material and preventive action has been taken to correct the process. Quality control will perform a first article inspection to verify that the process has been corrected. After acceptable CP action has been taken and verified, the quality engineer will approve the QCAN and the process can resume.

SUMMARY

The process control procedure provides guidelines for installing, executing, and sustaining SPC. It documents the history of the process; provides the rationale for selecting the charts, subgroups, frequencies, and so on; gives the criteria for out-of-control conditions; and provides specific instructions on what to do when out-of-control conditions exist. The procedure also defines and assigns accountability and has a mechanism for ensuring that the required actions are taken.

Once the process control procedure has been established, committed to, and effectively implemented by personnel, SPC will achieve the desired results.

9

Process Control Implementation*

Step 9, process control implementation, is the vehicle for implementing the process control procedure developed in Chap. 8. This is the final step of actually implementing SPC in an ongoing process. In steps 4–8 most of the team efforts were focused on problem solving, measuring the capability of the inspection system, determining the capability of the process, developing the process control procedure, and establishing the CP action matrix. Completion of this step will begin to internalize process control implementation and transform SPC into an everyday activity. Steps 10–12 are involved with the important follow-up activities after SPC has been implemented.

Step 9 is often referred to as the *do point*. It is the point where all previous activities are brought together and any incomplete activities are assigned to someone to do now. This is the action step where all of the team's carefully laid groundwork and plans are implemented. In this step the team

- Ensures that a checklist of prerequisites for SPC implementation are satisfactorily completed
- Provides the agenda for and conducts a preparation and coordination meeting
- Facilitates SPC implementation

---

* Ignacio Munoz participated in preparing this chapter, and Wendell Paulson participated in preparing the supplements.

Prerequisites for SPC Implementation

The team checks its plan by ensuring that the following seven prerequisites for implementing SPC are completed.

1. All individuals who will be using SPC must have satisfactorily completed a training seminar that at least explains why SPC is used, how to plot data on control charts, and how to interpret the data on the charts.

2. Step 5, IC study, must have been completed on the process where SPC will be implemented. The results of the study must indicate an acceptable capability.

3. Step 6, process capability study, must have been completed on the process where SPC will be implemented. The results of the study must indicate that the process is in control and that any process variation is due to chance causes (natural variation).

4. Step 7, CP action matrix, must have been developed for the process, approved by the team, and posted at the process operation.

5. Step 9, process control procedure, must have been written and approved in order to provide a system for introducing and maintaining SPC.

6. The events log must have been implemented. The log book should be located at or near the process where SPC is being implemented. It will contain entries about anything new, different, or changed in the process.

7. The control charts (see Chap. 9 supplements) that are selected for the operation must be posted at an approved location near the operation. Subgroup size and frequency must have been determined and approved. The ongoing center-line and control limits must also have been established and approved.

The Preparation and Coordination Meeting

The preparation and coordination meeting, as its name implies, coordinates the activities of personnel who will be implementing ongoing SPC. The results of previous studies should be discussed along with the methods used to bring the process under control. An in-depth review of the process control procedure should be undertaken. A clear understanding of step 9 is essential because it assigns responsibility for interpreting the control charts, for carrying out the actions on the CP action matrix, and for maintaining SPC on the process. Before the meeting ends, everyone should know who has responsibility for each activity. The team leader sees to it that all responsibilities are assigned.

Facilitate SPC Implementation

At the time process control is implemented, the manager responsible for that production department will monitor the start-up and hold the gains. At this level the manager is the one who has the most to gain from successful SPC implementation, and is usually a team member of the team or steering committee.

Although responsibility for process control is no longer in its hands, the project team continues to ensure that process control responsibilities have been assigned, action to protect the gains has been taken, and a measurement system to determine the project performance has been developed.

At the production line where SPC is implemented the manager reviews the selection and frequency of samples for control chart subgroups, the calculation of subgroup data, and data plotted on the control charts. He or she also closely monitors the action taken on out-of-control conditions, the use of the CP action matrix, and entries in the events log.

SUMMARY

Step 9 is the catalyst of the 12-step process. All of the key players meet together and verify their assignments, complete unfinished business, review the progress, make sure all the prerequisites are finalized, and review the plan. After clarification the team takes the final action and implements its plan.

SUPPLEMENT 1
Control Chart Basics

Implementating SPC successfully requires the company to use and understand process control charts. These charts provide valuable information that can be used to reduce defects on a real-time basis. This section discusses control chart concepts and typical control chart types used by the team, and presents basic statistical concepts along with their corresponding formulas and examples. The major emphasis of this supplement is on calculating and plotting control chart data and identifying from the control charts when action is required on the process being monitored.

Statistical Concepts

Statistics is the branch of mathematics involved with collecting, classifying, interpreting, and presenting numerical data. Statistical methods are very effective in the control of manufacturing processes to prevent defects through the control chart method. Data from a series of small samples called *subgroups* are used to estimate where the process is centered and how much it is varying around the center. Data are obtained from these subgroups and plotted on the control chart to give a picture of how the process is behaving. Thus, two statistics that must be understood are those that measure the center (average) of the process and the variation of the process.

Average

The *average* of the process is an unknown value (parameter) estimated by the average (mean) of the sample. This sample value is the statistic. *Estimated* means that the value of the statistic will be close to the average of the process but will almost never be equal to the *actual* average.

The average of the sample is denoted by $\bar{X}$ (read "X-bar") and computed as follows:

$$\bar{X} = \frac{\Sigma X}{n} = \frac{\text{Sum of all readings}}{\text{Sample size}}$$

Example: The measurements on a sample of parts are 0.4, 0.7, 0.9, 0.7, 0.3. Find the average.

$$\bar{X} = \frac{0.4 + 0.7 + 0.9 + 0.7 + 0.3}{5} = \frac{3.0}{5} = 0.6$$

This value indicates where the center or average of the process is located.

If the sample size is 5, the computation of the average can be simplified as follows, because sample sizes of 5 are often used on $\bar{X}$ and R charts.

Step 1. Total the readings.

Step 2. Multiply the total by 2.

Step 3. Move the decimal point one place to the left.

Example: Using the same numbers as in the previous example, find the average.

Step 1. The total is 0.4 + 0.7 + 0.9 + 0.7 + 0.3 = 3.0.

Step 2. 3.0 × 2 = 6.0.

Step 3. Moving the decimal point one place to the left gives 0.60 as the average, the same value as before.

Variation

Any process, natural or fabricated, has variations: manufactured parts, for example, are not all the same size. The variation of individual items, however, is not predictable. Although the size of the next part from a process cannot be predicted precisely, the general range can be determined.

The *allowable* variation of parts in a process typically consists of a nominal dimension plus or minus an allowed tolerance. If a part has a specification of 2.500 ± 0.050, the nominal is 2.500 and the allowable variation is from 2.450 to 2.550. So the variation of the process must be quantified to determine if the specification is being met.

The amount of variation, spread, or dispersion of the values in a distribution of values must also be expressed by a numerical value. If the values are grouped close to the average, the value of the measure of variation should be small. If the values are widely dispersed or spread out from the average, the value of the measure of variation should be large.

Two statistics commonly used to quantify or measure variation are the range and the standard deviation.

Range

The *range* (R) is the simplest measure of variation to compute. With ranges of several small *samples* from a process, managers can estimate the variation of the *process* distribution. The $\bar{X}$ and R control charts use the average range to estimate the process variation. The formula for the range is

$$R = \text{Largest reading} - \text{Smallest reading}$$

Example: Find the range of the numbers 3, 3, 5, 6, 8.

$$R = 8 - 3 = 5$$

Standard deviation

The *standard deviation* (S) is another statistic commonly used by management to quantify the variation of a process. The standard deviation tells how much the data are dispersed or spread around the average. If a process has small variation, most of the data will be close to the average and the value of the standard deviation will be small. If a process has large variation, the data will be more spread out or more dispersed around the average and the value of the standard deviation will be large. The formula is

$$S = \sqrt{\Sigma(\overline{X} - X)^2/(n - 1)}$$

where n is the sample size.

Example: Compute the standard deviation for the numbers 0.4, 0.7, 0.9, 0.7, 0.3. Set up a table with three columns as shown in Table 9.1. Compute the values in each column and the sum of each column as shown.

$$\Sigma X = 3.0 \qquad \Sigma(\overline{X} - X) = 0 \qquad \Sigma(\overline{X} - X)^2 = 0.24$$

If the sample size is 5, then

$$\overline{X} = (\Sigma X)/n = 3.0 / 5 = 0.6$$

$$S = \sqrt{\Sigma(\overline{X} - X)^2/(n - 1)} = \sqrt{0.24/4} = \sqrt{0.06} = 0.245$$

Normal distribution

Most measurements from manufacturing processes fall into a pattern called a *normal distribution* (Fig. 9.1) or a bell-shaped curve. As the figure shows, 68% of all values will be within one standard deviation from the average, 95% within two standard deviations, and 99.7% within three standard deviations. So, almost all (99.7%) of the measurements in a manufacturing process will fall in a distribution that is within plus or minus three standard deviations from the average.

Estimating the process distribution

In a sample of 30 pieces suppose the average is 0.102 and the standard deviation is 0.0015. Suppose that the *specification* for the process is

TABLE 9.1   Computations for Standard Deviation

X	$\overline{X} - X$	$(\overline{X} - X)^2$
0.4	$0.4 - 0.6 = -0.2$	0.04
0.7	$0.7 - 0.6 = 0.1$	0.01
0.9	$0.9 - 0.6 = 0.3$	0.09
0.7	$0.7 - 0.6 = 0.1$	0.01
0.3	$0.3 - 0.6 = -0.3$	0.09

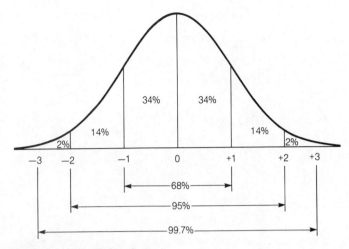

Figure 9.1 Normal distribution.

0.100 ± 0.010. Then the upper specification limit (USL) is 0.110, and the lower specification limit (LSL) is 0.090. The process can be pictured as shown in Fig. 9.2 with the average at 0.102. The -3σ value is 0.102 $-$ (3) (0.0015) = 0.0975, and the 3σ value is 0.102 + (3) (0.0015) = 0.1065. This process meets the specification, because it is well centered (process average of 0.102 compared to the specification nominal of 0.100) and the total variation (6σ = 0.009) is much less than the total specification spread (0.020). This example indicates that an ideal process is one where the average is the same as the specification nominal and the ± 3σ values do not exceed the upper and lower specification limits.

Consider a process that is producing a part with a specification of 0.625 to 0.665 on one dimension. The ideal process would have an average of 0.645, the $+3\sigma$ value would be 0.665, and the -3σ value would be 0.625. A picture of this ideal process is shown in Fig. 9.3.

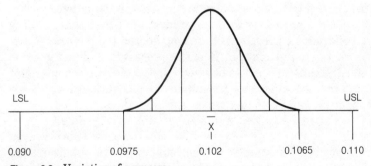

Figure 9.2 Variation of a process.

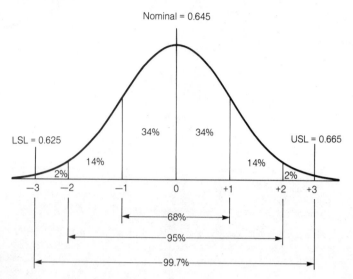

Figure 9.3 Ideal process.

Variable data and attribute data

The type of control chart selected depends on the type of data collected. Data collected for control charts can be classified as *variable* (generated from measurements of parts—e.g., length, thickness, width, diameter, hardness, resistance) and *attribute* (generated by counting defects or defectives—e.g., visual inspection, go/no-go gages, accept/reject decisions, drawing errors, invoice errors, and line item errors). Defects are defined as any nonconformity on a unit. Defectives are units with one or more defects.

Control Chart Concepts

The control chart is the statistical tool for implementing SPC. It provides information about a process, based on small samples (subgroups) periodically taken from the process. Each subgroup is a picture of what the process is doing or producing at that time. Taking successive subgroups corresponds to taking successive pictures of the process over time. Real-time control of the process is then achievable. However, for the control chart to be effective, the operator or inspector must obtain process samples for the subgroup, measure or inspect the parts immediately, and compute the subgroup values.

The samples must be gathered into subgroups with as small a variation as possible within the subgroup. This small variation is achieved by collecting consecutive samples for each subgroup. The subgroups are selected periodically (1 subgroup per half hour, 1 subgroup per hour, 1 subgroup per shift, 1 subgroup for every 200 pieces). The time between subgroups depends primarily on the production rate of the process.

For each subgroup a value is computed from the measurement data and plotted on the vertical axis of the control chart, as shown in Fig. 9.4. The horizontal axis represents time or the subgroup number.

When 20–25 subgroups of data have been obtained a center-line value and control limit values can be calculated. They are drawn on the chart, as shown in Fig. 9.5. If the process is in control, all the plotted points will be within the control limits. As long as the points fall within these limits the process is said to be in control, and no action is required. If a point falls outside the control limits, it is evidence that the process is out of control and corrective action is required. The cause of the out-of-control condition must then be found and removed.

When the process is in control, the variation of the values on the chart represents the *natural variation* of the process. This natural variation is a result of many elements that contribute equally and randomly to the variation. If the process is out of control, one of the elements in the process is causing excessive variation. Such an item is called an *assignable cause*. Assignable causes usually result from abnormal variations in the machine, material, people, method, measurement, or environment.

Control Chart Types

The type of control chart used depends on the type of data (variable or attribute) to be collected and plotted. Variable data are plotted on the average and range ($\bar{X}$ and R) chart. Attribute data are plotted on a p, np, c, or u chart. We will briefly describe the $\bar{X}$ and R, p, and c charts, which are the most commonly used in implementing SPC.

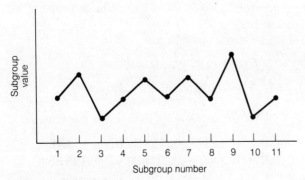

Figure 9.4 Control chart.

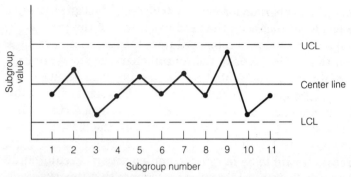

Figure 9.5   Control chart with center line and control limits.

$\overline{X}$ and R chart

The $\overline{X}$ and R chart is actually two control charts on the same form (see Fig. 9.6). For each subgroup the average $(\overline{X})$ and range (R) are calculated. The average of the $\overline{X}$'s is an estimate of the process average. The subgroup ranges are used to estimate the process variation or 6σ of the process.

The size of a subgroup is usually less than 10 pieces, with 4 or 5 being the most common, and should always be kept constant. How frequently subgroups are selected from the process is mainly a function of the production rate and process stability: The time between selections is less for a process with a high production rate. See Chap. 6 for more details.

The formulas and factors for computing the center line and control limits are shown in Table 6.1. A sample calculation follows. (We recommend that 20–25 subgroups be plotted on the chart before center line and control limits are calculated.)

Suppose 15 subgroups of size 5 have been obtained from a process and the shear force has been determined for each part. From the data, the average range is computed to be 39.67 lbs. and the average of all subgroup averages (center line) is 129.87 lbs.

The R chart control limits are

$$\text{UCL}_R = D_4\overline{R} = (2.114)(39.67) = 83.86$$
$$\text{LCL}_R = D_3\overline{R} = (0)(39.67) = 0$$

The $\overline{X}$ chart control limits are

$$\text{UCL} = \overline{\overline{X}} + A_2\overline{R} = 129.87 + (0.577)(39.67) = 152.76$$
$$\text{LCL} = \overline{\overline{X}} - A_2\overline{R} = 129.87 - (0.577)(39.67) = 106.98$$

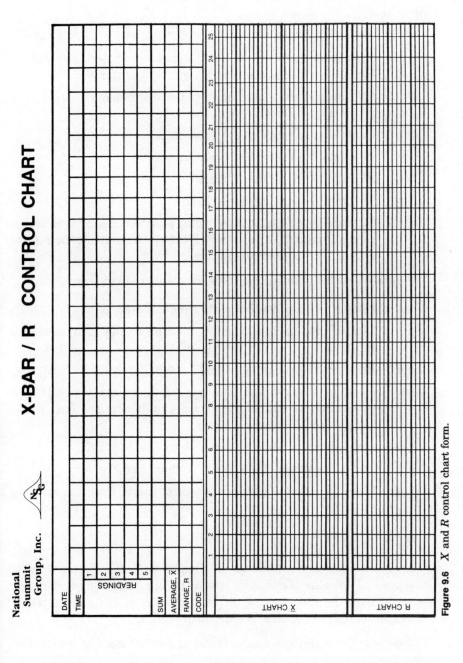

Figure 9.6 $\overline{X}$ and R control chart form.

Figure 9.7 shows the data plotted on an $\bar{X}$ and R chart. The process is in control.

To compute and plot data on the $\bar{X}$ and R chart, follow these steps:

Step 1. Select consecutive pieces for the subgroup. Select them "as is" before any touch-up or rework by the operator.

Step 2. Measure the parts and record the measurements on the appropriate data recording form.

Step 3. Compute the range of the subgroup.

Step 4. Compute the average of the subgroup.

Step 5. Plot the range on the R chart.

Step 6. Plot the average on the $\bar{X}$ chart.

Step 7. Interpret the results. If the point is within the control limits, continue running the process. If the point is outside the control limits, take appropriate action.

Example: Let us follow these steps for a subgroup of size 5.

Step 1. Obtain five consecutive parts from the process.

Step 2. Measure the parts and record the data on the form, as shown in Fig. 9.8.

Step 3. Compute the range: $R = 0.822 - 0.818 = 0.004$.

Step 4. Compute the average. The total of the readings is 4.100, so $(4.100)(2) = 8.200$. Moving the decimal point one place to the left gives 0.820 as the average.

Step 5. Plot the range 0.004 on the R chart (see Fig. 9.8).

Step 6. Plot the average 0.820 on the $\bar{X}$ chart (see Fig. 9.8).

Step 7. Since the point is within the control limits, continue running the process.

p Chart

The p chart is used to control the fraction or proportion defective (p) of a process. The value of p is computed by dividing the number of defective units in the subgroup by the total number of units inspected in the subgroup. It is usually recorded as a decimal.

Example: One defective unit is found in a subgroup of 50 units. The fraction or proportion defective is $p = 1/50 = 0.02$. The percent defective is thus $0.02 \times 100 = 2\%$.

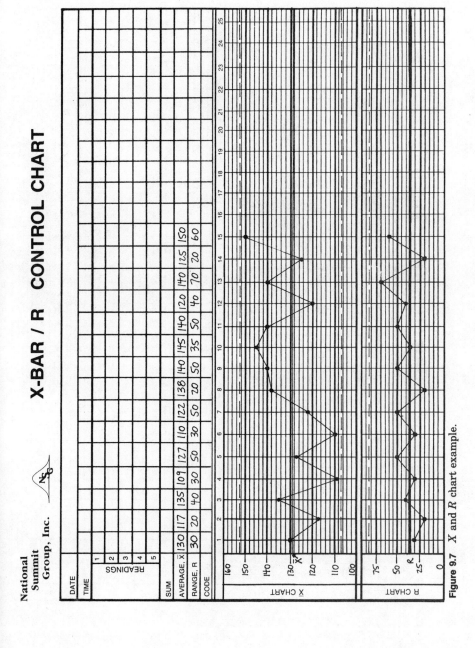

Figure 9.7 X and R chart example.

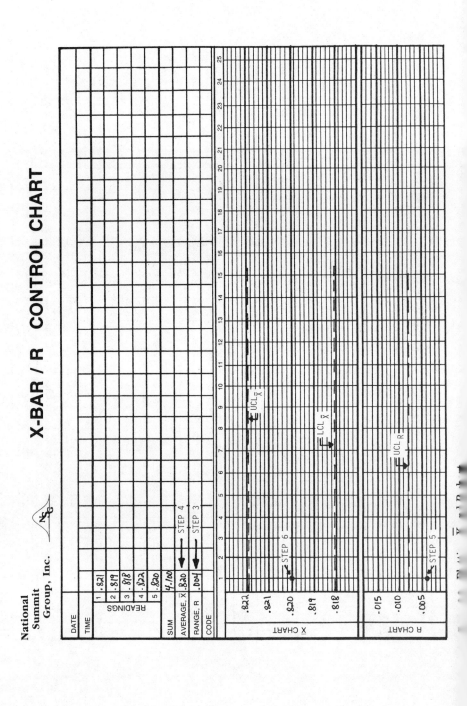

National
Summit
Group, Inc.

X-BAR / R CONTROL CHART

162

To make the computation and interpretation easier, keep the size of each subgroup the same (e.g., the number of parts produced in one day or in one shift), usually 25–100 (50 is recommended). Otherwise you must calculate a separate pair of control limits for each subgroup size. Unequal subgroup sizes can occur when the results of 100% inspection are plotted.

A p chart form is shown in Fig. 9.9. A completed p chart is shown in Figure 9.10. The formulas and calculations used to fill in this chart follow.

Suppose 25 subgroups of size 200 are obtained from a process, and the number of defectives and the fraction defective for each subgroup are recorded.

The center line is

$$\bar{p} = \frac{\text{Total number of defectives}}{\text{Total inspected}} = \frac{66}{(200)(25)} = \frac{66}{5000} = 0.0132$$

The control limits are

$$UCL = p + 3\sqrt{\frac{\bar{p}(1-\bar{p})}{n}} = 0.0132 + 3\sqrt{\frac{(0.0132)(0.9868)}{200}}$$

$$= 0.0132 + 3(0.0081) = 0.0132 + 0.0243 = 0.0375 = 0.038$$

$$LCL = p - 3\sqrt{\frac{\bar{p}(1-\bar{p})}{n}} = 0.0132 - 3(0.0081)$$

$$= 0.0132 - 0.0243 = -0.0111$$

Use LCL = 0 since LCL is less than 0.

To compute and plot data on the p chart, follow these steps:

Step 1. Select consecutive pieces for the subgroup from the process. Select them "as is" before any touch-up or rework by the operator.

Step 2. Inspect the parts. Count and record the number of defective parts on the appropriate data recording form.

Step 3. Compute *p*.

$$p = \frac{\text{Total number of defectives in the subgroup}}{\text{Subgroup size}}$$

Step 4. Plot *p* on the chart.

Step 5. Interpret the results. If the point is within the control limits, continue running the process. If the point is outside the control limits, take the appropriate action.

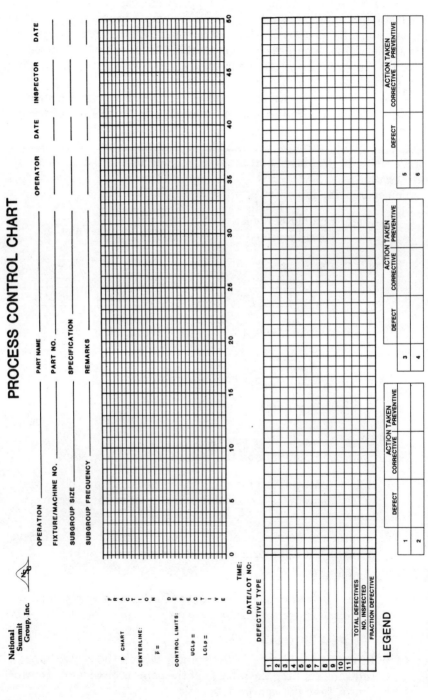

Figure 9.9 p Control chart form.

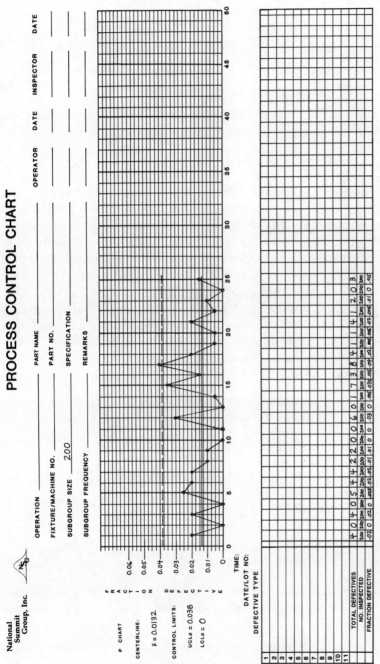

Figure 9.10 p Chart example.

Example: Let us follow these steps for a subgroup of size 200.

Step 1. Obtain 200 consecutive parts from the process.

Step 2. Inspect the parts. Suppose four defectives are found.

Step 3. Compute p: $p = 4/200 = 0.02$ (2%).

Step 4. Plot 0.02 on the chart (see Fig. 9.11).

Step 5. Since the point is within the control limits, continue running the process.

c Chart

The c chart is used to control the number of defects or nonconformities (c) in a process. The chart is used when numerous characteristics are inspected and the total number of defects could be large.

Subgroup sizes are usually small (1–5) and must be constant, or else the u chart must be used (see Fig. 9.12). Since it is possible to have more than one defect in each unit, it is also possible that the count of defects, c, per subgroup will be larger than the size of the subgroup.

A c chart form is shown in Fig. 9.13. A completed c chart is shown in Fig. 9.14. The formulas and calculations used to fill in this chart follow.

Suppose 18 subgroups of size 5 are obtained from a process and the number of defects for each subgroup is recorded.

The center line is

$$\bar{c} = \frac{\text{Total number of defects}}{\text{Total number of subgroups}} = \frac{20}{18} = 1.11$$

The control limits are

$$\text{UCL} = \bar{c} + 3\sqrt{\bar{c}} = 1.11 + 3(1.053) = 1.11 + 3.16 = 4.27$$

$$\text{LCL} = \bar{c} - 3\sqrt{\bar{c}} = 1.11 - 3(1.053) = 1.11 - 3.16 = -2.05$$

Use LCL = 0 since LCL is less than 0.

To compute and plot data on the c chart, follow these steps:

Step 1. Select consecutive pieces for the subgroup from the process. Select them "as is" before any touch-up or rework by the operator.

Step 2. Inspect the parts. Count and record the number of defects on the appropriate data recording form.

Step 3. Plot the number of defects in the subgroup (c) on the chart.

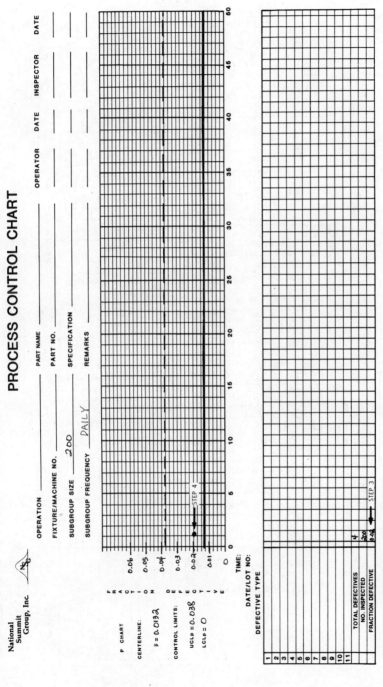

Figure 9.11 Plotting p chart.

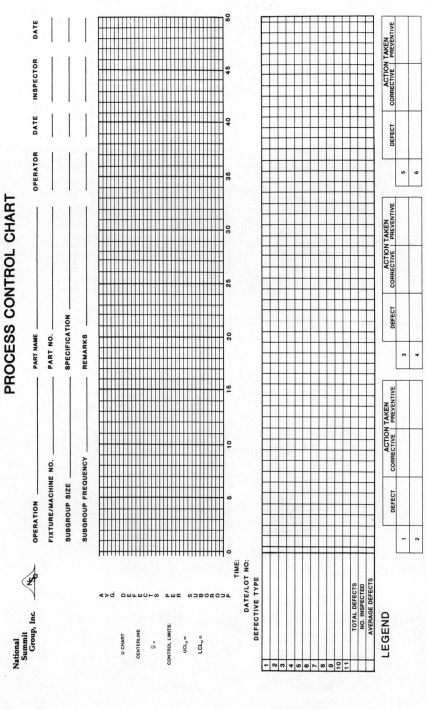

Figure 9.12 u Control chart form.

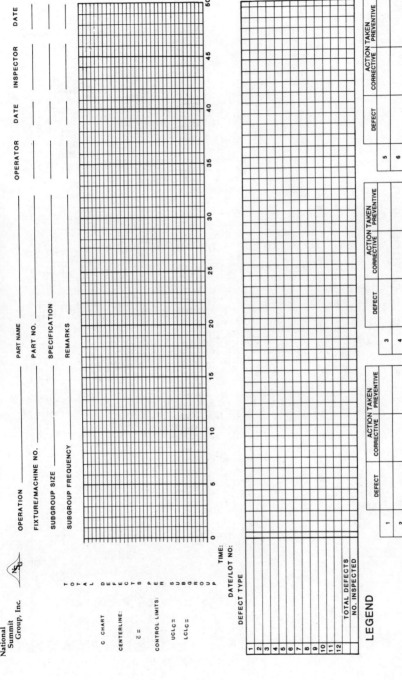

Figure 9.13 c Control chart form.

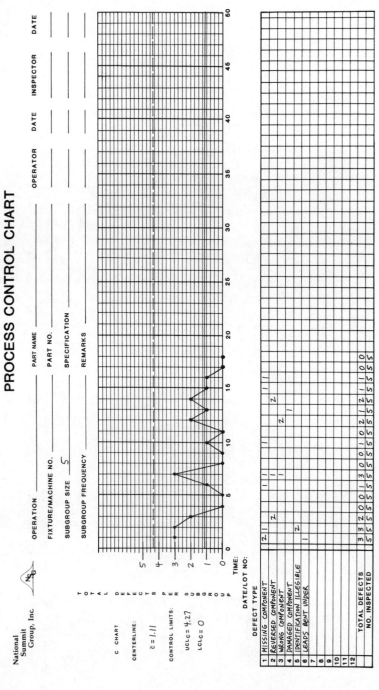

Figure 9.14 c Chart example.

Step 4. Interpret the results. If the point is within the control limits, continue running the process. If the point is outside the control limits, take the appropriate action.

Example: Let us follow these steps for a subgroup of size 5.

Step 1. Obtain 5 consecutive parts from the process.

Step 2. Inspect the parts. Assume three defects are found.

Step 3. Plot the number of defects, 3, on the chart (Fig. 9.15).

Step 4. Since the point is within the control limits, continue running the process.

Control Chart Interpretation

If the process is in control (all points within control limits), no action is taken. If the process is out of control (one point outside the control limits), the cause must be found and corrected.

Even if all points are within the control limits, a process may still be out of control if the points appear in a definite pattern. For example, seven points in a row appearing above or below the center line but not beyond the UCL indicate that the process has shifted. This type of pattern is called a *shift*. Corrective action should be taken when the seventh point occurs, before defective parts are made. This test should be used in a critical process in addition to the usual control limits.

Another pattern is seven points in a row upward or downward with no change in direction. This pattern is called a *trend*. Action should be taken when the seventh point is observed. These patterns are shown in Fig. 8.4, parts *d, e,* and *j.*

SUPPLEMENT 2
Implementation Guidelines

Process Flow Diagram for Production Processes

After the team has the knowledge and understanding of SPC concepts and methods, its first step in implementing SPC is to prepare a flow diagram of the process to determine the critical locations that require process control charts. The flow diagram shows the processes that collectively or sequentially produce the final product or document.

To prepare the process flow diagram, the team visits different locations, observes activities, and interviews key people. The team indi-

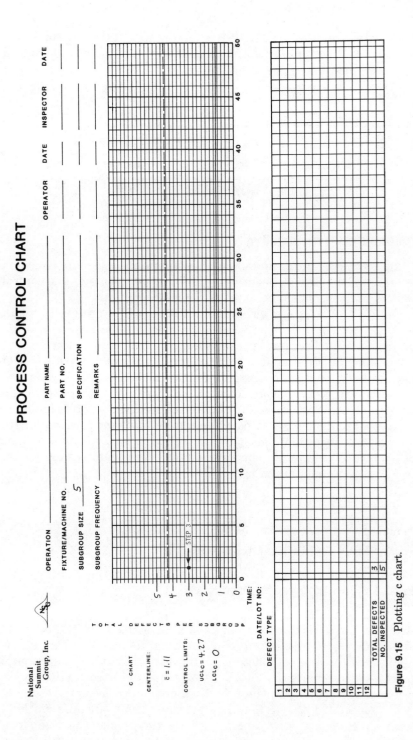

Figure 9.15 Plotting c chart.

cates the important items or characteristics to be checked or inspected at each inspection and appraisal point.

The usual flow diagram symbols are shown in Figs. 1.2 and 1.3.

SPC Implementation Conditions

It is not unusual for a company to have trained the right people in SPC concepts and methods but to have implemented little of SPC. The portion of SPC that was implemented probably achieved less than acceptable results. Management may proudly talk about its SPC program, when in fact it has only "quality veneer"—that is, the company appears to have implemented SPC, but it has not.

This section discusses guidelines for implementing SPC that will help the project team to prevent many problems during the critical implementation phase and to protect against quality veneer.

The first guideline requires the project team to review the process flow diagram for accuracy and applicability and, if necessary, modify it or create a new one. (See Chap. 1.)

The other guidelines are given as 11 conditions, with precepts, procedures, and illustrative examples.

Condition 1. Redundant factors exist in a process.

Definition. A *redundant factor* in a process is an input variable that exists in two or more physical quantities (e.g., machines, fixtures, operators, mold cavities, machine heads, materials).

Precept. When a redundant factor exists in a process, the team must obtain evidence that each item is in a state of SPC. When SPC exists and the process averages of each item are comparable and acceptable, the items can be consolidated on one control chart or kept on individual charts with a lower frequency of subgroup sampling.

Procedure:

1. If the process average being measured does not meet the quality specification requirement and the redundant factors are considered a significant source of the defects, then
   a. Conduct an IC study on the measurement or appraisal of the defects.
   b. Conduct a process capability study on each redundant factor.
2. If the process is not in SPC for any factor, then identify the assignable cause and take the appropriate CP action.
3. When each chart is in SPC and the process averages are comparable, then

    a. Reduce the frequency of subgroups taken for each individual factor or

    b. Consolidate all factors on a single control chart.

4. If one or more factors are not in control or the process averages are not comparable, then consolidate those that *are* in control and comparable on one chart and monitor the others on separate charts.

5. If more than one redundant factor is consolidated on a single control chart, then the source of the individual factors must be coded in order to provide an audit trail from the plotted point to the individual item.

Example: (see Fig. 9.16). A process that bonds a product to a critical thickness dimension of 0.850 ± 0.003 had two redundant factors: (1) 29 fixtures and (2) nine operators working in teams of three operators each. The production rate was nine per hour, and the reject rate was 27%.

When all the fixtures were plotted on a control chart, the process was found to be not capable. The strategy for correction included an IC study, a process capability study for each fixture, and an assignment of fixtures to each team.

Outcome. The IC studies were acceptable. The 29 fixtures were plotted on separate control charts; seven were immediately found to be out of control and pulled from the process. They were inspected, were deter-

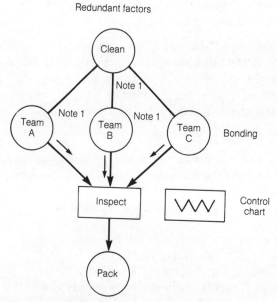

Figure 9.16   Redundant factors in a process.

mined to be out of specification, and were reworked. When the seven fixtures were returned to the process, the reject rate dropped to less than 0.5%. The 29 fixtures were then plotted on one control chart and coded by fixture identification number.

Condition 2. Redundant factors exist in previous processes.

Definition. A *redundant factor in a previous process* is an element that exists in two or more physical quantities in a process preceding the one being measured (e.g., two vendors, two or more operators or machines performing the same operation).

Precept. When the process being studied is out of control and a cause-and-effect diagram identifies a critical factor from a previous process, then the team should analyze that factor for redundancy and, if multiple items do exist, obtain evidence that each item (where that factor exists) is in a state of SPC. Once they are in control and the process averages of each item are comparable and acceptable, the items can be consolidated on one control chart or kept on individual charts with a lower frequency of subgroup sampling.

Procedure:

1. If the redundant factor is considered to be a significant source of defects, then
   a. Conduct a cause-and-effect-diagram study
   b. Conduct a process capability study for each item where that factor exists
2. Repeat procedural steps 2–5 for principle 1

Example: (see Fig. 9.17). Three grinding machines were charted separately on $\bar{X}$ and R charts, which showed all machines to be consistently out of control, with a reject rate of 24%. A cause-and-effect diagram indicated that hand removal of welding flash was a critical previous process performed by five operators per shift, who all fed their completed parts one by one into a consolidated grand lot.

Individual control charts were installed for the five operators, and it was found that one, a new employee, was out of control. In addition, although the other four operators were in a state of SPC, a significant difference in the process average was observed among them, which made frequent machine adjustments necessary.

A solution to the problem required each operator to collect his or her own parts and supply them to the grinding machines with lot integrity traceable to each operator. The results were that an out-of-control condition for a grinding machine occurred only occasionally (at the initial setup of each lot) and rejects dropped from 24% to less than 2%, with a corresponding increase in productivity of 18%.

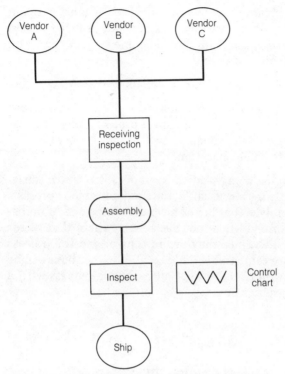

Figure 9.17   Redundant factors in a previous process.

Condition 3.   During a process capability study, plot data on the control chart immediately.

Requirements.   Plot data on the control chart immediately upon collecting and inspecting the subgroups. Do not wait until 25 subgroups (which are required to calculate control limits) are collected.

Precept.   Major problems can be identified, interpreted, and, occasionally, solved after observing the first few data points. Control limits are not always needed to identify obvious problem-solving situations. Problem solving should start when obviously unfavorable data points are seen (e.g., when the level of percent defects, or defects per 1000 or freaks, is higher than expected).

Procedure:

1. Plot data on the chart as they are collected.
2. Observe the data for freak readings, significant trends, or unreasonable data. Any nonrandom pattern or unusual level of rejects may indicate an out-of-control condition. Look only for the obvious.

3. If freak readings, significant trends, or unreasonable data are observed, initiate the problem-solving techniques at once.

Example: A u chart was installed to plot defects per unit area in a painting process for a large piece of radar equipment. The first five points plotted were 25, 37, 31, 28, and 52. It was obvious to the operators that their performance was unacceptable. The charts highlighted the rejects that no one had focused on before.

After observing the five unusual points, of which only one point per week was plotted, the operators investigated their process and recommended changes, such as increase the lighting, keep the doors closed during painting, and overhaul the paint nozzle.

Outcome. The operators' recommendations produced an 87% decrease in defects, and productivity increased from 72 to 94%. Recall that improvements were initiated after only five data points were plotted on the chart.

Condition 4. Multiple cause-systems for a process.

Definition. A *multiple cause-system* for a process is one in which the process has two or more mutually exclusive cause-systems. A *cause-system* is a subset of one or more related processes that could create specific defects or errors. These defects are cause-and-effect related to the subset.

In other words, a multiple cause-system exists where the various defects are mutually exclusive and related to a particular subset of a process but not to all the processes feeding into the location where the subgroup is being collected.

Precept. When a multiple cause-system for a process exists, the team must obtain evidence that each cause-system is in a state of SPC and has acceptable process averages. When that state exists, the cause-systems can be consolidated to one control chart at the appropriate location, or the frequency of collecting subgroups for individual charts may be reduced.

Procedure:

1. When a process is not capable but is in control and the process average is unacceptable, then separate the cause-systems.

2. Conduct an IC study on the measurement and appraisal of the defects.

3. Conduct a process capability study for each cause-system. Address the causes for the defects and provide solutions. Maintain the charts until they are in a state of SPC and their process averages are acceptable.

4. Consolidate the favorable cause-systems on one chart, or reduce the subgroup sampling frequency. Should any of the cause-systems be out of control, or have an unacceptable process average, maintain them on separate charts and conduct problem solving until they are in control and acceptable.

Example: This control chart reflects five cause-systems: purchased parts (defective) coded A, a hand-stuff process (predominantly workmanship) coded B, a variable component device (VCD) machine process coded C, a dual in-line package (DIP) machine process coded E, and a solder process coded F.

A process capability study was conducted for each specific cause-system because the composite process was in control but its process averages were unacceptable.

A control chart was installed at hand-stuff where the actual name or part number of the wrong part, misinstalled part, or missing part was recorded and fed back to the operators. Additional charts were installed for the DIP and VCD machines and after the solder process. The separate charts allowed the precise cause or symptom to be monitored, whereas grouped data did not provide adequate information for problem solving.

After the causes of defects of each cause-system were addressed and in control and their process averages were acceptable, the subgroup frequency was decreased and the cause-systems were consolidated on one chart. The point plotted for each cause-system was coded in order to have an audit trail back to the precise cause-system.

Outcome. The process control chart for purchased parts defects initiated preventive action at the suppliers, resulting in fewer rejects. The chart for hand-stuff proved its defect level was almost 0.

The control chart for the DIP machine initiated action to rework tooling plates, which removed the cause of error. The chart for VCD machines indicated that the cut-and-clinch operation was not functioning repeatably; it was repaired and the cause of defects was removed. Charts for the solder process immediately identified the wrong type of solder in the process at recurring times; this was corrected and the cause for defects was removed.

Condition 5. Real-time feedback.

Definition. Real-time feedback means that immediately after the parts are produced, the subgroup is collected, parts are inspected, and the point is plotted on the chart. The results are immediately fed back to the process operators.

Precept. Real-time feedback is mandatory for successful SPC. Delays in communication may cause excessive defects and a tendency to merely *detect* defects rather than *prevent* them. The communication time lapse should not be greater than the time required to collect the subgroup, inspect the parts, and plot the data.

Procedure:

1. Post the control charts, events log, and CP action matrix in a prominent location that is visible to operators of the cause-system being monitored.
2. Record subgroup data on the control chart as soon as the inspection and test are completed.
3. Immediately take the prescribed action indicated by the CP action matrix.
4. Audit the process to ensure compliance.

Example: This process involved several repair operators who worked on drilling units. A day or two later, inspectors would find an average of three defects per subgroup.

The solution was to change the inspection procedure so that the inspector took random samples from repair personnel immediately after the units were repaired. Each repairer's work was identified and separated from the others. The random sampling was determined by rolling a die and inspecting at a frequency of 1 out of 5. It was then possible to plot a chart for each repairer as soon as completed units were available, and to immediately feed the results back to the individuals.

Outcome. Rejects dropped to an insignificant level after the high-reject repairers were identified, trained, and tested on their knowledge of acceptance criteria.

Condition 6. Families of product with equal opportunity.

Definition. *Families of product with equal opportunity* is a model of products that possess similar or equal opportunities for defects. Opportunities for defects are considered equal when the differences are within a 20% range. For example, a machined plate with 100 holes could be grouped with one of 120 holes and another of 110 holes.

Precept. Consolidate models on one chart for a process capability study when their opportunities for defects are within a 20% difference.

Procedure:

1. Method 1: Use multiple charts.
   a. Count the number of opportunities for defects on the various models of product and compare the models to each other.
   b. If they are within 20% of each other, group them in a family.

   c. State on the chart which models are authorized to be plotted.

   d. When grouping two or more models, code each model and note the code on the chart.

2. Method 2: Use a u chart and extrapolate the defects to defects per 1000 or defects per 1,000,000 opportunities.

   a. Count the opportunities.

   b. Extrapolate the defects per *x* opportunities.

   c. Code the point for the specific model.

Example of multiple charts by family

Model	No. of opportunities for defects
A (simple)	250
B (complex)	400
C (medium)	318
D (simple)	170
E (simple)	200
F (complex)	500

Outcome. Eight separate charts can be consolidated to three by using this technique.

Condition 7. Provide a detailed description of defects for c and p charts.

Precept. Clearly describe the defective, including part type or part number, and set priorities for the defects.

Procedure. Describe the defect.

Examples of descriptions

Wrong:	Defective parts (e.g., wrong diameter).
Right:	Give the part number or name of the defective and, if possible, state the defect [e.g., diameter too large (.304)].
Wrong:	Improper part.
Right:	List the defect (e.g., reversed polarity, wrong part, broken part, damaged part, not inserted, or missing parts).

A separate checksheet can be used to record the defect type and its frequency.

Condition 8. Use consecutively produced parts as subgroups (variable and attribute charts).

Precept. Consecutively produced parts provide minimum variation within subgroups. The time between subgroup selections or quantity of parts among subgroups provides maximum variation between subgroups.

Procedure. Collect and inspect n consecutive parts and plot the data on the appropriate chart.

Example: An $\bar{X}$ and R control chart was installed on a drilling machine. Five consecutive parts at a time were collected and inspected, and the data were plotted. It was observed then that the R chart frequently went out of control.

Outcome. Problem solving uncovered that the bearing holding the drill bit was worn. It was replaced, and the process returned to an in-control condition.

Condition 9. Review the R chart first, then the $\bar{X}$ chart.

Precept. The R chart should be in control before setting control limits on the $\bar{X}$ chart. Large swings in range (dispersion) may mask the true process mean. The cause of excessive ranges must be corrected prior to addressing the $\bar{X}$ chart.

Condition 10. A process in a state of SPC does not always produce acceptable parts at the desired level.

Precept. Compare subgroups against specifications. If all are acceptable, continue as normal. If two or more parts are defective, address the defect with the appropriate problem-solving technique. Remember that the investment in time to solve the problem must provide a return in terms of meeting the customer's requirements or in dollar savings.

Procedure. Compare part measurements from the variable control chart to the specification; for attribute charts compare the process average to the quality targets. If parts are being produced with one or more defective parts in a subgroup, then take the following actions:

1. Set priorities for the defects.
2. Take appropriate action from the CP action matrix.
3. Refer to the events log for possible causes.
4. Compare the existing conditions to those when the process capability study was run; look for changes. If a process capability study was not run, conduct one.
5. Conduct a diagnostic process audit.
6. Conduct a cause analysis if the process has changed.
7. Construct a cause-and-effect diagram if it is a new problem.

8. Conduct a designed experiment if applicable.

9. Using a Pareto analysis, constantly address the highest defect until the quality level is acceptable to the customer.

Condition 11. The $\bar{X}$ and R chart is the most powerful (sensitive) type of control chart.

Precept. Use the $\bar{X}$ and R chart for critical characteristics and characteristics with high defect rates. Continue charting this way until confident that the process is under control. Then either reduce the inspection frequency, or record the characteristic on an attribute chart.

Procedure:

1. Change from go/no-go attribute inspection to variable-data inspection methods.

2. Plot the specific measurements on an $\bar{X}$ and R chart.

3. Use appropriate problem-solving techniques.

4. When the process is under control, reduce the subgroup frequency or record the characteristics on an attribute chart.

Example: A process requiring inspection of belt tension used a go/no-go gage to measure the tension. The instrument was then changed to one with a measured reading, and data were plotted on an $\bar{X}$ and R chart. The results of the R chart indicated that there was significant variability in the measuring instrument.

Outcome. A new measuring instrument was used and the defects were eliminated. The R chart indicated that the instrument was consistently out of control. The new instrument indicated when the process went out of control, and preventive action was exercised to correct the situation.

Alternative. If an instrument with a measured reading is not available, then in some cases the operator could make a judgment call relative to a process: for example, with a tape die-cutting process, the operator could call the cut excellent, acceptable, or poor. Then a logical rating could be given to the operator's evaluation, such as 5 for excellent, 3 for acceptable, and 1 for poor. Then an $\bar{X}$ and R chart could be developed with this rating system, which could help evaluate the process.

To determine if quality veneer exists in the operation, use one or more of the following tests:

1. Is it a real-time system? Are characteristics measured immediately after the process?

2. Are charts plotted and information fed back to the operator immediately?

3. Are the process input parameters charted so that the process rather than the product is controlled?

4. Are the control charts posted near the operator's or user's process?

5. Are the out-of-control conditions noted with some type of action or attention on the chart?

If the answer to any or all of these questions is no, then there is the real probability that only "quality control reporting with control limits" exists. SPC's only value then is for reporting detection, not prevention. Control charts turn into wallpaper with little value, and SPC will only serve the system rather than create outstanding results. Education, training, serious implementation of the steps discussed in this book, application of the 11 guidelines, and a commitment to success will avoid quality veneer and produce the expected results.

Problem Prevention*

Problem prevention, step 10 in the PQI process, is a method for controlling critical factors that can lead to future problems. Frequently, improvement projects cease as soon as the original problem has been resolved or the initial objective has been met. Opportunities for further improvement in the process are usually overlooked. The need to prevent problems is just as critical as the need to solve them.

For example, a manufacturer of printed circuit boards reduced the number of defects per board from an average of 7 to 3.5 at the conclusion of step 9. The process was meeting the objective of 50% improvement established in step 1, and the process was in a state of statistical control. In order to continue its success, the company also looked at potential future problems. The resulting projections and actions taken not only prevented future problems but reduced the defects per board from 3.5 to 1.5.

Problem prevention is concerned with the design and implementation of two very important activities: *preventive action,* which reduces the probability of occurrence of a problem due to controllable causes— it removes the cause before it becomes a problem—and *contingent action,* which minimizes the impact of the problem when it occurs; it is an action for an uncontrollable cause or a cause where preventive action is not feasible or economical.

A problem prevention plan must

1. Identify potential critical problems and determine if they are controllable

---

*Stephen Wernick and Ignacio Munoz participated in preparing this chapter.

2. Identify the likely causes of the critical problems
3. Identify preventive actions to address the causes
4. Implement preventive actions
5. Prepare contingent actions
6. Identify a "triggering mechanism" for contingent actions

The interrelationships of the actions are illustrated in Fig. 10.1.

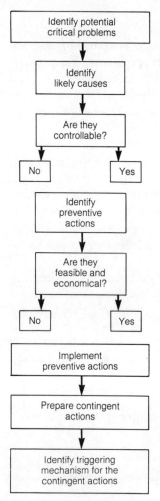

Figure 10.1 Problem prevention process flow diagram.

Identify Potential Critical Problems

It is likely that many of the potential problems to be identified will be those that were investigated while solving the original problem in step 4 of the PQI process. In the printed-circuit-board-assembly example given earlier, the original problem concerned component preparation. Other problems investigated included solderability, damaged components, wrong components, and contamination. These other problems would then be identified as likely potential problems.

The team can identify additional problems by asking what problems have surfaced in the past and what problems may affect performance in the future. Depending on the complexity, criticality, or impact of the problem on the desired objective, the team may generate an extensive list of potential problems. However, not all potential problems are critical, so there is no need to address them all. The team must assign priorities to determine which problems need to be addressed immediately and which can be delayed. Record potential problems on the worksheet of Fig. 10.2.

Identify Likely Causes

Chapters 4 and 7 showed that many likely causes are possible for a given effect. The team must analyze each potential problem listed and its likely cause(s). The causes may be thought of in terms of influences or events that lead to the effect. Some of the likely causes of a potential problem may be unknown or not fully explained. In those cases the team might prepare a cause-and-effect diagram or use one of the other techniques of Chap. 4 to explore possible causes.

The list of likely causes will probably be extensive. Because it is not practical to identify and develop preventive actions for *every* likely cause, the causes should be listed in order of importance. The team should first determine if a cause is controllable—preventable. Machine breakdown, for example, can be prevented through an effective preventive maintenance program. On the other hand, problems caused by adverse weather conditions are, in most cases, uncontrollable. Since preventive action usually does not exist for uncontrollable causes, the team need not address them. The remaining likely causes should now be listed from most likely to least likely.

Identify Preventive Actions

Identify one or more preventive actions that will keep each likely cause from occurring. Preventing the cause from occurring prevents the problem (effect) from occurring.

Problem	Likely cause	Preventive action (PA)	Individual responsible for PA	Target completion date for PA	Contingent action	Alarm

Figure 10.2   Potential critical problems worksheet.

Analyze each preventive action for feasibility and expense. If the action is not feasible, it should not be considered. Every action has a cost and will require an allocation of resources in anticipation of some future return. The ideal action will yield a high return at a minimum cost. Consider the following rules before making a final decision:

Rule 1. A simple preventive action is a good investment when it significantly reduces the probability of addressing a critical problem in the future.

Rule 2. A complicated and expensive action is a poor investment when its purpose is to prevent a lesser problem that is unlikely to occur.

Implement Preventive Actions

A good implementation plan consists of a master plan and a detailed plan. The master plan contains all preventive actions selected, individual(s) responsible for their implementation, target completion dates, and follow-up dates. The detailed plan contains the individual activities required to implement the specific preventive actions.

Prepare Contingent Actions

In the process so far, some likely causes were dropped because they were uncontrollable and some preventive actions were decided against because they were impractical or expensive. So the process is still exposed to the potential problem. Also, no matter how well it is designed and implemented, the preventive action may not always be effective. To further minimize that exposure and lessen the impact of problems when they do occur, the team prepares contingent actions.

Developing contingent actions requires looking only at the potential problem without regard for its likely cause(s). Contingent action should not be confused with backup preventive action. For example, a desired end result might be to get to work on time. One potential problem could be that the car will not start. A likely cause is a dead battery, and the preventive action is to check the battery's charge periodically. The contingent action would be to take a cab. Notice that the contingent action applies regardless of the likely cause. Keeping an extra battery in the garage might be a contingent action, but it is impractical because the likely cause of the car not starting might be something else. So for every potential critical problem that is listed a corresponding contingent action must be prepared.

Identify Triggering Mechanisms or Alarms

Contingent actions are most effective when they are properly timed. For example, taking a cab would lead to the desired end result only if it were called at the right time. To ensure timely action, the team must establish a triggering mechanism or alarm. If this preparation is not made, the contingent action could be ineffective because the problem might be too far advanced. The contingency alarm clearly states that trouble has occurred, and the back-up action must be implemented *immediately*. In our example of the dead battery, the alarm might be "cables are securely fastened and radio won't go on."

Failure Mode Effect Analysis

Failure mode effect analysis (FMEA) is a method of problem prevention that can be carried out by design and reliability engineering in the early stages of product introduction. FMEA assigns the probability of failure and the probability of detection by use of a classification weight for each failure mode.

The FMEA technique is a structured method of design review that causes engineers to consider potential failure modes and to rank failure modes according to their impact on reliability. FMEA identifies problems that need immediate attention and defines preventive action that must be taken prior to release of a new design.

The procedure for FMEA is as follows:

1. Determine potential failure modes. This is clearly the most difficult step in the process and relies on engineering experience and historical data taken from other products or previous designs. It is necessary to consider what could go wrong with the part or assembly and what symptoms or effect on the product would be observed. In a radio, for example, one potential failure mode is that the speaker connection breaks. The effect of this failure is no sound.

2. Determine the most likely cause for each of the failure modes to be addressed. Any problem-solving technique discussed in problem analysis and solution may be applied at this point. There may be more than one cause for a given failure mode.

3. Estimate a probability of occurrence for each failure mode. To simplify this estimate, use a scale of 1 to 10, where 1 is the lowest probability of occurrence.

4. Estimate the relative weight or criticality of each failure mode. The team must consider safety, conformance to specification, product function, and customer satisfaction when assigning a relative weight. On the scale of 1 to 10, 1 is an incidental failure that is unlikely to

effect product performance or the customer's perception of quality; 10 is a critical failure that will cause personal injury or certain product failure.

5. Estimate the probability of escaped defects, again using the scale of 1 to 10. A perfect inspection station would catch all of the defects and would be rated 1 (low probability of escaped defects). This estimate may be derived from an IC study for a similar part.

6. Calculate a risk priority number by multiplying the factors determined in steps 3–5. The higher the risk priority number, the more important it is to find a cause and preventive action.

7. Identify appropriate preventive action that will eliminate the cause of the potential failure mode.

For example, suppose we were designing an automatic umbrella. For the sake of brevity, we will select only two potential failure modes: (1) fracture of the umbrella shaft in high-wind loads and (2) separation of the stitching of the umbrella fabric. The effect of the first failure would be catastrophic failure of the device. The second failure effect may range from a cosmetic problem to leaks.

As experienced umbrella engineers, we rate the likelihood of the first failure·mode at a 3 (not especially likely) and the second failure mode as 9 (almost always happens). The criticalities of the failure modes are rated as 9 and 5, respectively. The chance of finding a weak shaft at inspection is low and rated at 6, and the chance of catching bad stitching is very good and rated at 2. The form in Fig. 10.3 can be used to tabulate the results of our evaluation.

Notice that a fracture may occur in two ways. The shaft material may be thinner than specified, or the environmental conditions may exceed design expectations. Thin material is identified as the most significant problem. This example shows that failure modes and causes may be ranked by the risk priority number and addressed in order of significance.

Failure mode effect analysis is an excellent tool for design and reliability review and should be required in conjunction with reliability testing.

SUMMARY

A team can easily be lulled into a false sense of security after identifying the major problem and implementing solutions to address it. Problem prevention is a natural extension of problem analysis and problem solving. Preventive actions can be implemented at once to prevent

Failure Mode Effect Analysis

Part no. _____ 99-10001-01

Description _____ Umbrella

Test assembly _____ Top

Engineer _____

Date _____

Part name or number	Potential failure mode	Effect of failure	Cause of failure	Risk probabilities (scale of 1 to 10)			Risk priority no.	Preventive action
				Occurrence	Severity of failure	Escaped defects		
Umbrella shaft	Fracture	Umbrella not usable	1.Thin material, below specification	3	9	6	162	1. Specify thicker tubing for shaft Change to solid graphite shaft
			2.Umbrella caught in severe wind shear or microburst during thunderstorm	1	9	6	54	2. Print warning in owner's manual
Stitching	Separation	Rain leaks through seams; owner gets wet	1.Poor workmanship	9	5	2	90	1. Review operator training and workmanship manual

Figure 10.3   Failure mode effect analysis form.

most potential problems from occurring. Contingent actions are the backup measures that are already identified and can be quickly put to use if needed.

This step protects the successful results already achieved by the team, maintains project momentum, and enhances further quality and productivity improvements within the process.

Defect Accountability*

Defect accountability is a system for assigning responsibility for each defect or error identified in the process in a manufacturing, administrative, or service function.

For the team to assign responsibilities objectively it must first define the defects and collect data to determine where the defects are occurring. Data collection must be customized to the specific application. The process can be tedious, complex, and time consuming if not thought out carefully in advance. When designing the system, the team must consider where to collect data, how to collect data, how much data to collect, and how to process the data. Because there is no single best method for defect accountability, this decision is left to the data collector. This chapter covers these points.

Developing the defect accountability system involves (1) designing the data collection forms, (2) allocating defect responsibility, and (3) collecting the defect data. Before proceeding with the development of the system, let us review the sources and types of defects or errors.

A *defect* is defined as a nonconformity to a specification on an article. All defects can be categorized as (1) component, (2) design, (3) process, or (4) workmanship defects. If one did not know which category best fits a given defect, then the defect could be categorized as "miscellaneous" or "unknown."

Component defects result from the use of defective parts, components, or raw materials for which the operator is not responsible. This is usually the case when it is impossible to detect potential defects or when the cost of receiving inspection or prior inspections is prohibitive. Exam-

---

*Michael Millow and Ignacio Munoz participated in preparing this chapter.

ples of component defects are an integrated circuit that fails during testing of the final printed-circuit-board assembly, paper that creates illegible printing, and a piece of metal with excessive voids that cause pitting when machined.

Design defects are caused by a deficiency in the design. They generally cannot be compensated for practically or economically through process adjustments. Examples of design defects are inadequate clearance between holes and leads, which creates soldering problems, mating parts not matching due to tolerance stack-up, and functions that do not consistently repeat themselves.

Process defects are generated by the process through its methodology, tooling, or fixturing due to lack of repeatability. Although the operator followed the prescribed methodology, these defects occur because they are part of the normal variation of the process. Examples of process defects are insufficient solder due to temperature variability of the wave-solder-machine preheaters, rough surface finish due to tool wear, and damaged components caused by loose bearings in automatic assembly equipment.

Workmanship defects occur when the operator does not adhere to the production, test, or inspection method. Examples of workmanship defects are missing hardware or components from a hand-assembly process, and wrong components loaded onto a machine or assembled during hand assembly.

Designing the Data Collection Forms

Two types of data collection forms are required: the *defect summary sheet* and the *traveler*. These two documents are intended for multioperation processes, as in an assembly line. Less complex processes might vary from this chapter. In any event the forms must be customized to each process.

Defect summary sheet. The *defect summary sheet* serves as a single source document for keeping track of all defects found at an inspection station. It is also a guide for allocating defects to the responsible station, the last station assigned to prevent that defect. A summary sheet is required for each inspection station in the process.

1. *List all potential defects.* To design a defect summary sheet, begin by listing all the characteristics (defects) inspected at the station being addressed. Typically, these would be the defects manufactured since the last inspection point. It also may include random characteristics already inspected in order to maintain controls on previous inspection stations.

2. *Determine the responsible station.* Review each defect listed to determine its origin, that is, the most likely station generating the defect. The responsible station is the one at which the defect can most likely be prevented from recurring. Certain defects have dual responsibility assigned to them between production and inspection. This condition is called *inspection leakage.* These defects are characteristics that have already been inspected at a previous inspection point and missed. However, the defects were originally created by production.

3. *Determine the defect source.* Determine if the defect source is component, design, process, or workmanship.

4. *Record defects on the form.* The form should be simple but meaningful. Consider computerizing final reports, keeping documentation to a minimum, and matching data to units produced. Figure 11.1 is a sample form.

The traveler. The *traveler,* as the name implies, is a document that travels with the unit or lots of units produced. Although the traveler has many practical uses, this section discusses only how this document relates to the traceability and accountability of product quality. For illustration purposes, the traveler is designed to show the progress of one unit.

1. *Process flow diagram.* Prepare a process flow diagram identifying all operation, inspection, and material-handling steps. These steps should include all areas where defects can be generated or detected. The flow diagram is the road map for the traveler.

2. *Form design.* The traveler must contain all of the information in the sample in Fig. 11.2. This is the minimum information required. Other requirements may be added to suit the particular product or process being addressed.

Allocating Defect Responsibility

The proficiency in allocating responsibility for each defect determines the overall effectiveness of the program. To make the program implementation and execution easier, we recommend that all allocation be done when the defect summary sheet is designed, *not* as each defect is experienced. To accomplish this requires some knowledge of the process capability and manufacturing methods, including equipment, tooling, and fixturing requirements. For example, the first defect description on the defect summary sheet might be incorrect hole size on base. To allocate responsibility for the defect, first identify the station by name or number where the base is drilled. Enter the finding in the column headed responsible station. It is not always clear who is really respon-

Weekly Defect Summary Sheet

M   T   W   TH   F   Sa

Units   Operation no. _____
Inspected   Revision _____
Accepted   Week ending _____
Yield

Element no.	Defect description	Responsible station	Defect source	Number of defects					
				M	T	W	TH	F	Sa

Figure 11.1 Weekly defect summary sheet.

Traveler

Model _____   Date _____

Work order no.   Serial no. _____   Packed _____

Status

Station no.	Employee no.	Date	Disposition	Station no.	Employee no.	Date	Disposition
010				120			
020				130			
030				140			
040				150			
050				155			
055				160			
100				195			
110				200			

Rejection and Repair History

Rejected by	Defect element no.	Accountable station	Accountable employee	Source of defect	Description of defect	Repaired by	Reinspected by

Figure 11.2   Traveler.

sible. Even in this example, we could argue that the base-drilling station is not really responsible for the defect—after all, it might have no control over the setup of the equipment or the raw materials used. The key factor, however, is that this is the station where the defect was created and first observed. Therefore, when determining responsibility, select the station most likely to originate the defect.

If the defect is one that has already been inspected at a previous inspection station, the responsibility should be assigned equally to the inspection station for allowing it to leak through and to the operation that created the defect. This condition is commonly found in an assembly line or similar continuous process where there are several inspection stations throughout the process. Knowing the station where the problem is originating is not sufficient information to effect adequate CP action. The *source* of the defect must be established.

Next, determine the source of the defect—workmanship, process, component, or design. Ask the following questions:

1. Can this defect be avoided when the operator follows the approved production method?

2. Can the defect be avoided through better methods, tooling, fixtures, or equipment?

3. Are the characteristics of the components such that dimensional stability is difficult to achieve?

4. Could any changes be economically made to the process or component to compensate for the defect?

If the answer to question 1 is yes, the defect source is workmanship. Reducing workmanship errors is one of the most challenging management tasks. About 80% of workmanship errors are the fault of management. A worker is accountable for an error if the following conditions are met:

1. The operator must have detailed instructions, preferably with sketches, for performing his or her assigned task and know what acceptable quality is

2. The operator must have thorough training, preferably by a professional trainer or supervisor, to perform the assigned task and to know if he or she is accomplishing what is expected

3. The operator must have all necessary tools and equipment

4. The operator must have the means to regulate the process if his or her performance is not meeting expectation, providing it is within the detailed instructions

If any one of these conditions is not met, management is accountable for the error, and engineering (a management support function) must determine the defect source.

Workmanship errors can be classified as (1) unintentional, (2) method, or (3) intentional. Analytical methods for determining the types of errors include the person/error type matrix, which displays the errors of several people and the respective types of errors, and is the most useful analytical method; Pareto analysis, which separates the "vital few from the trivial many" for each person; and trend analysis, which examines the consistency of each operator over time.

Unintentional errors occur because the operator is unable to continually be attentive to the task. He or she is unaware of having made an error. Hence such errors are unpredictable—there is no pattern as to the type of error, who will commit it, or when it will be committed. To prevent unintentional errors, management must (a) in some way help the operator remain attentive; (b) foolproof the operation to reduce its dependence on the operator; (c) make the errors "problems of the day" until they are resolved.

Methods errors occur because the operator lacks some essential technique, skill, or knowledge. Management must determine which of these essentials is lacking and provide tools or training to eliminate the errors. Otherwise the operator must be replaced.

Intentional errors are deliberately committed by the operator, who consistently makes them. He or she may do this because of real or imagined grievances against the company or supervision.

(There is also a class of intentional errors that is inadvertently management-induced. These can be caused by shifting priorities among cost, delivery, productivity, and quality. They can also be caused by inadequate communication. (1) A product with errors is passed from one department to another. The person receiving the product thus assumes it is all right to use. (2) Supervisors post charts showing if projects are on schedule, but none showing if the projects are meeting quality standards. (3) Supervisors launch a poster campaign on doing better work. Although most errors can be controlled by management, the campaign makes no provision to improve the quality of purchased parts, subassemblies, process capability, and machine maintenance. The message comes across as "Do as we say, not as we do."

Management can take the following actions to eliminate intentional errors:

1. Make the operator aware of the impact the error has on other work or on the customer
2. Assign the error to an operator who is accountable for the error, thus providing ownership of the process

3. Enhance the supervisor's impact because people mirror their supervisor's behavior pattern and will emphasize quality, schedule, and productivity as the supervisor does

4. Conduct process audits on operators and inspectors and product audits on inspectors

5. Assign the most demanding work to operators with the best performance records

If the answer to question 2 on page 200 is yes, then the source of the defect is the process. As with workmanship defects, it is tempting to allocate more defects to the process than are appropriate. A good process makes the operation idiotproof, compensates for mediocre designs, and weeds out bad components only if there are unlimited resources, engineering time, money, and a customer willing to wait for that process to be created. For example, the process might lack controls to ensure the repeatability of the operation, and preinspecting every hole might be too expensive. To arrive at the best decision, use collective expertise. If it is not reasonable and justifiable to expect the process to prevent these defects, proceed to the next source.

If the answer to question 3 is yes, then components are the source of the defect. Components can be anything from basic commodities to major subassemblies, depending on the stage of the process where the inspection occurs. For example, a component of a printed-circuit-board assembly might be a capacitor, and that assembly would be a subassembly of the final product. Components are purchased materials and they may come from a supplier without (external) or within (internal) the company. As long as there is room for error as a tradeoff for lower costs (98% acceptable product, 4% acceptable quality level, etc.), there will always be component errors in the product. Management must maintain control over these defects and isolate the most critical or repetitive.

If the answer to question 4 is no, then product design is the source of the defect.

Collecting Defect Data

Now that the defects to be inspected are identified, their source and responsible station are determined, and the necessary forms are designed, the next step is to implement those elements and begin the data collection. The primary tool for data collection is the traveler. The traveler is issued to the first production station along with all the materials required for that operation. The traveler contains the work order number, model, serial number, and date.

Each operator or inspector working on the product is responsible for entering the necessary information next to the station number for which he or she is responsible.

1. Status section—self-explanatory.
2. Rejection and repair history section
   a. Enter the employee number of the inspector finding the discrepancy.
   b. Enter the defect element number from the weekly defect summary sheet. If the particular defect is not listed, enter "random." Random defects may be planned or unplanned. An *unplanned random defect* is one that is not listed or is not part of the inspection or test instruction for that station but is detected during normal tests or inspection. A *planned random defect* is one that the inspector has been instructed to inspect or test on a sampling basis, usually for a limited time. Planned random defects are usually not significant enough to check regularly and are not part of the normal process: for example, a defect generated from an alternative process that is used because the primary process is down.
   c. Enter the accountable station according to the weekly defect summary sheet. If the defect was random and not listed, investigate its origin.
   d. Enter the accountable employee number from the status section of the traveler. For example, if the defect element number indicates that this defect is critical at station 030, then go to the status section and find out the number of the employee who worked at station 030 when the unit was produced. If the defect was random, determine who was responsible while investigating the responsible station.
   e. Enter the source of the defect from the weekly defect summary sheet. If the defect was random, determine the source while investigating the accountable station.
   f. Briefly and clearly describe the defect. Give its exact location.
   g. Enter the employee number of the individual repairing the defective unit.
   h. Enter the employee number of the individual inspecting the unit.

SUMMARY

Defect accountability is a reporting system used to further segregate problem areas on an ongoing basis in order to generate continued improvement and sustain the gains already made by the team. The primary objectives of defect accountability are to

1. Report defects based on their source (process, component, design, workmanship)

2. Identify acceptable and nonacceptable operators and inspectors

3. Identify acceptable and nonacceptable component sources

Defect accountability does not stop with defect identification and assignment of responsibilities. The team must finally develop a program or ensure that one is in place to recognize and reward outstanding individuals who are participating in and contributing to the success of the PQI process. Employees have accepted the responsibility for their own process and defects, so they should be rewarded for exceptional achievements. There should also be a formal program for coaching or handling individuals with less than satisfactory performance, to bring them up to the same level as the outstanding performers.

Programs of this type may vary significantly from company to company, depending on their individual culture and policies. Sometimes this program is coupled with or is a part of an existing performance appraisal system.

Measurement of Effectiveness*

Measurement of effectiveness is not only the last step of the 12-step PQI process, but it is also the step that cycles back to step 1. Step 12 involves audits that measure the improvement achieved and identifies further opportunities. Before the project is closed, one or more audits are performed to see how well the team carried out the objectives of productivity and quality improvement defined in step 1. Audits also assess overall implementation of the techniques. This chapter discusses product, process, systems, and financial audits and how to conduct them.

Product Audits

Product audits verify the performance level of the process by measuring the output of the process. The purpose of the audit is to ensure that the outgoing quality of the product is consistent with the project objectives. This audit involves inspecting a sample of the output that was previously accepted by the normal acceptance process. The audit results are then compared with the normal acceptance results and with the project quality objectives.

Product audits can be implemented at an in-process point or in the final stages of a process. A final audit of a manufactured product may be performed before or after the product has been packaged.

---

*Ignacio Munoz participated in preparing this chapter.

Process Audits

Process audits verify proper implementation of changes to the process and provide assurance that the process documentation, equipment, and necessary support are still current and consistent with the improvements made in steps 1–11. Its primary objective is to ensure that the gains made and reported by the team will be maintained after the project is closed.

The process audit specifically checks the adequacy of the process documentation and the conformance of the manufacturing personnel with the process methods and procedures. It also provides assurance that the process documentation, tools, and material support have been kept current for optimum producibility.

The recommended checklists to be used in the audit are displayed in Fig. 12.1.

Systems Audits

Systems audits verify that the respective organizations have implemented and maintained the process control procedure. The primary objectives of this audit, as in the process audit, are to ensure that the gains made will be sustained after closure of the project and to ensure the stability of the process over time. A checklist for conducting this audit is given in Fig. 12.2.

Financial Audits

Financial audits verify that the projected savings of the project were actually achieved. The audit reviews financial reports with the accounting department to identify actual dollars saved compared to the dollars projected in step 1. The savings will usually appear in reduced rework costs, quality appraisal costs, warranty and repair costs, increased labor efficiency and expenditures relating to the project (such as the cost of project implementation).

Conducting the Audit

Although measurement of effectiveness is the team's responsibility, a member of the steering committee should accompany the audit team as an observer to ensure objectivity of the results. Table 12.1 lists the appropriate committee member for each type of audit. Note that the team leader is responsible for coordinating the audit and for the following actions.

Process Audit Checklist

Plant: _____   Date: _____

Product or area: _____   Auditor: _____

Station: _____   Operator: _____

Documentation: Part I

No.	Document description	Availability Yes	No	Comments
1.	Assembly instructions			
2.	Inspection instructions			
3.	Workmanship standards			
4.	Calibration procedure			
5.	Test instructions			
6.	Fabrication methods			
7.	Station layout			
8.	Training records			
9.	Product specification			
10.	Tooling drawings			

Figure 12.1 Process audit checklist.

Process Audit Checklist

Plant: _____   Date: _____

Product or area: _____   Auditor: _____

Station: _____   Operator: _____

Documentation: Part II

Element no.	Element description	Verification* A	M	U	Diagnostic* A	M	U	Comments
1.	Are documents complete?							
2.	Are documents clear?							
3.	Are documents correct?							
4.	Are operations in proper sequence?							
5.	Are rework and reinspect instructions included?							
6.	Are interactions included for defects to be reinspected?							
7.	What is the latest DCO revision?							
8.	Are reference documents included where applicable?							
9.	Are necessary support documents available? (For example, variations, work-manship-standards photographs, sketches, minimum acceptable samples, etc.)							
10.	Does the manufacturing instruction adequately address all quality issues called for on the inspection instruction?							
11.	Does the inspection instruction adequately represent the product specification and workmanship standard?							

* A=acceptable, M=marginal, U=unacceptable.

Figure 12.1 *(Continued)*

Process Audit Checklist

Plant: _____   Date: _____

Product or area: _____   Auditor: _____

Station: _____   Operator: _____

Human Factors
(Operators and Inspectors)

Element no.	Element description	Verification* A	M	U	Diagnostic* A	M	U	Comments
1.	Has the operator or inspector been given skills training or job training? Has the operator been tested on skills and knowledge? By whom? Method?							
2.	Can the physical elements of the process be accomplished by the operator or inspector?							
3.	What is the operator's or inspector's attitude toward adequacy of the documentation?							
4.	Are working conditions conducive to quality workmanship?							

* A=acceptable, M=marginal, U=unacceptable.

Figure 12.1 *(Continued)*

Process Audit Checklist

Plant: _____   Date: _____

Product or area: _____   Auditor: _____

Station: _____   Operator: _____

Station Layout

Element no.	Element description	Verification* A	M	U	Diagnostic* A	M	U	Comments
1.	Does the station location conform to the area floor plan?							
2.	Does the station physically conform to station layout plan?							
3.	Is the station identified by number of the function or operation performed?							
4.	Is general housekeeping maintained?							
5.	Are safety practices adhered to?							

* A=acceptable, M=marginal, U=unacceptable.

Figure 12.1 *(Continued)*

Process Audit Checklist

Plant: _____   Date: _____

Product or area: _____   Auditor: _____

Station: _____   Operator: _____

Operation

Element no.	Element description	Verification*			Diagnostic*			Comments
		A	M	U	A	M	U	
1.	Are process documents present? (For example, manufacturing method, inspection instructions, test instructions, etc.)							
2.	Is document revision status correct?							
3.	Do the documents reflect the master copy? (No unauthorized changes.)							
4.	Is setup done according to instructions? (For example, machine, work station, etc.)							
5.	Are required tools and gages available at the station?							
6.	Are tools and gages in good working order? Are calibration stickers current where applicable?							
7.	Does the operator or inspector perform the operation exactly according to the process documents?							
8.	Does the operator or inspector follow the sequence prescribed by the method?							
9.	Does the operator or inspector properly utilize tools and equipment?							

* A=acceptable, M=marginal, U=unacceptable.

Figure 12.1 (*Continued*)

Systems Audit Checklist

Plant: _____   Date: _____

Product or area: _____   Auditor: _____

Station: _____   Operator: _____

Data Collection at Inspection and Test Station

Element no.	Element description	Verification*			Diagnostic*			Comments
		A	M	U	A	M	U	
1.	Are the control charts posted? Clearly visible? Properly labeled?							
2.	Are the data on the control charts current to today's date?							
3.	Are actions for out-of-control points indicated in the legend?							
4.	Are signatures of supervisors and engineers on the control chart?							
5.	Are center lines and control limits on chart? If $\bar{X}$ and R chart, on both charts?							
6.	Is there a corrective and preventive action matrix current?							
7.	Are the PQI teams following an inspection and test process control procedure?							

* A=acceptable, M=marginal, U=unacceptable.

Figure 12.2 Systems audit checklist.

TABLE 12.1   Steering Committee Representatives to Each Type of Audit

	Steering committee representatives	
Type of audit	Primary	Secondary
Product	Quality manager	Engineering manager
Systems	Manufacturing manager	Quality manager
Financial	Finance manager	Manufacturing manager
Process	Engineering manager	Manufacturing manager

1. Plan and prepare the audit
   a. Establishes the date when the team will have the first 11 steps fully implemented and documented according to the requirements of the respective step and be ready to be audited by the steering committee
   b. Notifies the respective steering committee representative and schedules the audit
   c. Obtains and prepares all applicable checklists
   d. Obtains and reviews necessary documentation
2. Perform the audit
   a. Notifies area supervisor of the audit on the day of the audit (not necessary for financial audits)
   b. Introduces the audit team to the supervisor(s), operator(s), and inspector(s) of the area to be audited, explains the purpose of the audit, and instructs personnel to follow their normal procedure
   c. Conducts the audit using the appropriate checklist(s)
   d. Records audit findings as acceptable, marginal, or unacceptable (the steering committee member can help make these decisions)
3. Measure effectiveness
   a. Reviews and assesses the results of the audit and issues a report that summarizes the findings
   b. Reviews all marginal and unacceptable results and identifies corrective action for each, using the audit corrective action summary report sheet (Fig. 12.3) to document the specific actions, responsibilities, and target dates for resolution
   c. Recommends closure or continuation of the project to the steering committee, based on the findings of the audit: for the audit to be successful and the project closed, at least 90% of the elements audited must fall in the acceptable range and an approved corrective action plan must exist
   d. Recommends further improvement to the process, product, or related processes and products if required

Audit Corrective Action Summary Report

Audit date: _____

Operation: _____

Auditors: _____

Line and station: _____

Item no.	Deficiency and probable cause	Action to be taken	Individual responsible	Target date	Action status and comments

Figure 12.3 Audit corrective action summary report form.

SUMMARY

This step completes the 12-step PQI process and determines the success of the team's effort. If the 12 steps are successful, the team may now recommend closure of the project to the steering committee and move on to the next project. After SPC is implemented, the process will be monitored and various actions will be taken until the original objectives are achieved and sustained. As a final action the team should look beyond its original objectives and view the process output as it relates to customer requirements.

Quality Targets*

This appendix, though not one of the 12 steps, is recommended to completely close the loop. Once SPC has been implemented the process should be improved to a level that meets customer requirements. Customer quality requirements are usually expressed as the maximum fraction or percent defective allowed—that is, the number of defects per opportunities divided by the number produced. For example, a customer may require that the product contain no more than 1% defective when shipped. The most cost-effective way to meet this requirement is to establish quality targets for each step in the process, with the final target being the customer requirement. Then the final product will meet the customer's need without extensive internal inspection or sorting.

This appendix describes a method for calculating quality targets, including target principles, sequences of inspection and test stations, target computations, and product flow versus quality flow. Like SPC, quality targets is 90% management action and 10% statistics. Quality targets *without* management action is actually detrimental to the efforts of PQI. To be effective, quality targets must be accompanied by a plan and subsequent management action.

The plan contains logical, reasonable, and sequential actions that must be taken to move the quality level from where it is to the new level, the names of responsible individuals, the target date chosen by the responsible individual and accepted by the team leader, and the follow-up date for the team leader. The plan must be distributed to the individuals responsible for action and to their respective managers and must be documented and updated periodically.

If the quality target is significantly different from the existing quality level, the targets must be incrementally "stepped" with subtargets in between.

---

* Wendell Paulson participated in preparing this chapter.

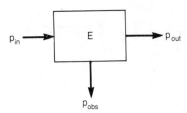

Figure A.1   Basic 100% inspection and test station model. E = effectiveness. $p_{in} = p_{out} + p_{obs}$. $p_{out} = p_{obs}(1 - E)/E$. $p_{obs} = p_{out} [E/(1 - E)]$.

The real secret to success is transforming these actions into results. The actual transformation is not within the scope of this section; it is a learned skill. The most effective way an individual learns it is by making a commitment to obtaining the education and having access to demonstration, coaching, reinforcement, and feedback from a person skilled in developing such learners.

The quality target for each step in the process is the maximum outgoing quality level allowed at each inspection and test point in the process (receiving to shipping). The targets and requirements will be expressed as a fraction defective. Thus a 5% defective requirement or target will be expressed as 0.05 fraction defective.

Target Principles

The computation of targets begins with a basic model developed around a 100% inspection and test station as shown in Fig. A.1. Incoming quality is denoted by p_{in}. It is the defective rate coming into the station from previous inspection station(s) or manufacturing operation(s). Mathematically, $p_{in} = p_{obs} + p_{out}$. Outgoing quality is denoted by p_{out}. It shows the defective rate going out of the station after the inspection and testing is complete. Effectiveness is denoted by E and is a measure of how good the inspection and test are in detecting nonconforming parts: $E = p_{obs}/p_{in}$ ranges from 0 to 1. If $E = 1$, then effectiveness is perfect and p_{out} is 0. Further, p_{obs} will equal p_{in}. If $E = 0$, then p_{obs} is zero and $p_{out} = p_{in}$. Observed quality is denoted by p_{obs}. This is the defective rate observed at each inspection and test station. It is computed from the inspection and test results and is reported to management as the quality level at that inspection and test station.

The outgoing quality of any inspection and test station is

$$p_{out} = p_{obs} (1 - E)/E \qquad (A.1)$$

Equation (A.1) uses the observed quality at the inspection and test station, which is always known from inspection results, and the effectiveness E. The effectiveness is determined from an IC study (see Chap. 5).

Example: Let $p_{obs} = 0.08$ (8%) and $E = 0.8$. Find p_{in} and p_{out}.

$$p_{out} = p_{obs}(1 - E)/E = 0.08(1 - 0.8)/0.8$$
$$= 0.08(0.2/0.8) = 0.08(\tfrac{1}{4})$$
$$= 0.02 (2\%)$$
$$p_{in} = p_{obs}/E = 0.08/0.8 = 0.10 \quad (10\%)$$

These formulas assume that any rework or reinspection and retest performed on defective material is 100% effective and does not introduce any new defective parts. This assumption simplifies the computations and results in calculated target values that are tighter than required.

The following observations are made about the basic model to make the formulas easier to apply.

- The outgoing quality of an inspection and test station is never observed in practice. It can only be determined by a special audit or by feedback from the next station or from the customer.

- The outgoing quality of an inspection and test station is the incoming quality of the following inspection and test station.

- When the observed quality is 0, either the effectiveness is 0 or the defective rate has improved to 0. When this occurs, perform an audit to determine if the outgoing quality is really 0 or if the effectiveness might be 0.

Sequences of Inspection and Test Stations

To establish targets for each inspection and test station, management must develop methods to determine outgoing quality levels for a sequence of stations. These methods will depend on whether the stations inspect and test completely different characteristics (case 1), the same characteristics (case 2), or a combination of characteristics (case 3).

The methods described here consider only two stations for simplicity.

Case 1. Two inspection and test stations checking different characteristics.

In this case, the stations are referred to as *mutually exclusive* stations. The outgoing quality from these stations is the sum of the outgoing quality from each station, as shown in Fig. A.2. The value of the outgoing quality from both inspection and test stations, p_{out}, is

$$p_{out} = p_{out\ 1} + p_{out\ 2}$$

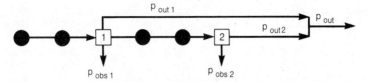

Figure A.2 Two inspection and test stations checking different character-istics.

Example: Let station 1 have $E = 0.8$ and $p_{obs} = 4\%$, station 2 have $E = 0.9$ and $p_{obs} = 3\%$. For station 1, $p_{out\ 1}$ is from Eq. (A.1),

$$p_{out\ 1} = p_{obs}\ (1 - E)/E$$

$$= 0.04\ (1 - 0.8)/0.8$$

$$= 0.04\ 0.2/0.8\ = 0.04\ (\tfrac{1}{4})$$

$$= 0.01\quad(1\%)$$

For station 2, $p_{out\ 2}$ is

$$p_{out\ 2} = p_{obs}\ (1 - E)/E$$

$$= 0.03\ (1 - 0.9)/0.9$$

$$= 0.03\ 0.1/0.9\ = 0.03(\tfrac{1}{9})$$

$$= 0.0033\quad(0.33\%)$$

The final outgoing quality from both stations is

$$p_{out} = p_{out\ 1} + p_{out\ 2} = 0.01 + 0.0033 = 0.0133\quad(1.3\%)$$

Case 2. Two inspection and test stations checking the same charac-teristics.

This instance is the same as 200% inspection, and the outgoing qual-ity from the second station is a function of the observed quality at the first station and the effectiveness of the two stations combined as shown in Fig. A.3.

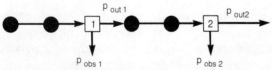

Figure A.3 Two inspection and test stations checking the same characteristics.

The equation for computing the outgoing quality of station 2, $p_{out\ 2}$, is

$$p_{out\ 2} = p_{obs\ 1}\ (1 - E1)\ (1 - E2)/E1$$

where E_1 is the effectiveness of station 1
E_2 is the effectiveness of station 2
$p_{obs\ 1}$ is the observed quality at station 1

Thus the outgoing quality of station 1, $p_{out\ 1}$, equals the incoming quality of station 2, $p_{in\ 2}$.

Example: For station 1 let $E_1 = 0.80$ and $p_{obs\ 1} = 25\%$ (0.25); for station 2 let $E_2 = 0.90$. The outgoing quality of station 2, $p_{out\ 2}$, is

$$p_{out\ 2} = p_{obs\ 1}\ (1 - E_1)\ (1 - E_2)/E_1$$

$$= 0.25\ (1 - 0.80)\ (1 - 0.90)/0.80$$

$$= 0.25\ (0.20)\ (0.10)/0.80$$

$$= (0.25)\ (0.02)/0.80 = (0.25)\ 0.025$$

$$= 0.00625\quad (0.625\%)$$

With 200% inspection and test, the incoming quality at station 1 is "sorted down" to 0.62%.

Case 3. Two inspection and test stations checking some characteristics that are different and some that are the same.

The final outgoing quality from station 2 is the sum of the outgoing qualities resulting from the different characteristics checked at each station and from the same characteristics checked at both stations.

We have

$$p_{out\ 2} = p_{out\ 1A} + p_{out\ 2A} + p_{out\ 2B}$$

where 1A are the characteristics checked only at station 1
2A are the characteristics checked only at station 2
2B are the characteristics checked at both stations

Example: Suppose station 1 has $E_1 = 0.80$, $p_{obs\ 1A} = 0.02$, and $p_{obs\ 1B} = 0.04$. 1A and 1B are two sets of characteristics, where set 1B is checked again at station 2 by set 2B. Suppose station 2 has $E_2 = 0.90$ and $p_{obs\ 2A} = 0.03$. Compute the outgoing quality for the set of characteristics, 1A, checked only at station 1:

$$p_{out\ 1A} = p_{obs\ 1A}\ (1 - E_1)/E_1$$

$$= 0.02\ (1 - 0.8)/0.8$$

$$= 0.02\ (0.2/0.8) = 0.02(\tfrac{1}{4}) = 0.005\quad (0.5\%)$$

Compute the outgoing quality for the set of characteristics, 2A, checked only at station 2:

$$p_{\text{out 2A}} = p_{\text{obs 2A}} (1 - E_2)/E_1$$

$$= 0.03 (1 - 0.9)/0.9$$

$$= 0.03 (0.1/0.9) = 0.0033 \quad (0.33\%)$$

Compute the outgoing quality at station 2 for the characteristics checked at both stations:

$$p_{\text{out 2B}} = p_{\text{obs 1B}} (1 - E_1) (1 - E_2)/E_1$$

$$= 0.04 (1 - 0.80) (1 - 0.90)/0.80$$

$$= 0.04 (0.20) (0.10)/0.80$$

$$= 0.04 (0.02)/0.80 = (0.04) 0.025$$

$$= 0.001 \quad (0.1\%)$$

The outgoing quality for all characteristics at station 2 is

$$p_{\text{out 2}} = p_{\text{put 1A}} + p_{\text{out 2A}} + p_{\text{out 2B}}$$

$$= 0.005 + 0.0033 + 0.001$$

$$= 0.0093 \quad (0.93\%)$$

Target Computations

To meet customer quality requirements, the maximum outgoing quality levels (maximum defective) allowed from each station must be established and met. In particular, this level must be controlled at each station by establishing individual targets for it. The target is the maximum value of the observed quality at each station that cannot be exceeded in order to meet the quality requirements of the next station.

The quality target at each station is

$$\text{Target} = p_{\text{MOQA}} [E/(1 - E)] \tag{A.2}$$

where p_{MOQA} is the maximum outgoing quality allowed from a station. The model in Fig. A.1 is then modified as in Fig. A.4.

Example: Suppose the maximum outgoing quality allowed for a particular station is 2%, and that $E = 0.8$. Then

$$\text{Target} = p_{\text{MOQA}} [E/(1 - E)]$$

$$= 0.02 [0.8/(1 - 0.8)] = 0.02 (0.8/0.2)$$

$$= 0.02 (4) = 0.08 \quad (8\%)$$

Note that the target value is larger than the outgoing quality allowed. This occurs because a 100% inspection and test station is being used and the quality is being sorted. Keeping the observed quality under 8% will ensure that the outgoing quality from the station does not exceed 2%. Targets for a sequence of stations can be computed as follows.

Case 1. Two inspection and test stations checking different characteristics.

The target must be computed for each station from Eq. (A.2). Since the final outgoing quality is the sum of the outgoing qualities from both stations, the maximum outgoing quality allowed must be divided between the two stations. Two methods are presented for allocating the maximum outgoing quality allowed between the two stations. The method used depends on whether there is any previous quality history.

Method for no previous quality history available. This method is based on the number of characteristics being checked at each station. Allocate the maximum outgoing quality allowed by the proportional number of characteristics being inspected at each station.

Example. Suppose two stations are inspecting different characteristics, with station 1 checking 10 characteristics and station 2 checking 20. Suppose the maximum outgoing quality allowed from these two stations is 0.03 (3%).

Determine the maximum outgoing quality allowed from each station as follows: A total of 30 characteristics are inspected: 10 or 33% at station 1, and 20 or 67% at station 2. Allocate the 3% allowed from these two stations as follows: 33% (⅓) of 3% to station 1 = 1%; 67% (⅔) of 3% to station 2 = 2%.

Method for previous quality history available. Allocate the maximum outgoing quality allowed proportionally to the quality history (percent defective) for each inspection station.

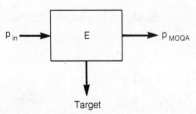

Target

Figure A.4 Target at 100% inspection and test model. MOQA = maximum outgoing quality allowed. Target = $p_{\text{MOQA}}[E/(1 - E)]$.

Example. Suppose two inspection stations are inspecting different characteristics with a maximum outgoing quality allowed of 3%. Suppose the previous quality history is station 1, 0.04 or 4%; station 2, 0.02 or 2%.

Determine the maximum outgoing quality allowed for each station as follows: The total percent defective from the two stations is 6%: 4% or 67% of the total from station 1, and 2% or 33% of the total from station 2. Allocate the required quality target of 3% as follows, based on the previous quality history: 67% (⅔) of 3% to station 1 = 2%; 33% (⅓) of 3% to station 2 = 1%.

Case 1 Example: Suppose two inspection stations are inspecting different characteristics and that the maximum outgoing quality allowed from the two stations is 0.03 or 3%. Suppose further that the quality history is available for each station and is the same as the previous example, with 4% from station 1 and 2% from station 2. Let the effectiveness be 0.8 for station 1 and 0.85 for station 2.

Determine the targets for each station as follows: The maximum outgoing quality allowed from both stations is divided between the two stations according to the prior quality levels. Two-thirds of the target or 2% is assigned to station 1, and one-third or 1% of the total is assigned to station 2. The maximum outgoing quality allowed from station 1 is $p_{\text{MOQA 1}} = 0.02$. The maximum outgoing quality allowed from station 2 is $p_{\text{MOQA 2}} = 0.01$. From Eq. (A.2), for station 1,

$$\text{Target}_1 = p_{\text{MOQA 1}} E_1/(1 - E_1)$$

$$= 0.02 \ [0.8/(1 - 0.8)] = 0.02 \ (0.8/0.2)$$

$$= 0.02(4) = 0.08 \quad (8\%)$$

For station 2,

$$\text{Target}_2 = p_{\text{MOQA 2}} E_2/(1 - E_2)$$

$$= 0.01 \ [0.9/(1 - 0.9)] = 0.01 \ (0.9/0.1)$$

$$= (0.01)(9) = 0.09 \quad (9\%)$$

Case 2. Two inspection and test stations checking the same characteristics.
Thus

$$\text{Target}_1 = p_{\text{MOQA 2}} \ [E_1/(1 - E_1) \ (1 - E_2)]$$

$$\text{Target}_2 = p_{\text{MOQA 2}} \ [E_2/(1 - E_2)]$$

Case 2 Example: Suppose two final inspection stations are inspecting the same characteristics. Suppose the maximum outgoing quality allowed from both stations is 0.02 (2%). Since both stations check the same characteristics, the maximum outgoing quality allowed from station 2 is 2% (MOQA 2 = 0.02). Suppose the effectiveness for each station has been determined to be $E_1 = 0.80$ or 80%, $E_2 = 0.85$ or 85%. Then

$$\text{Target}_1 = p_{\text{MOQA 2}} \times [E_1/(1 - E_1)(1 - E_2)]$$

$$= 0.02 \, [0.8/(1 - 0.8)(1 - 0.85)]$$

$$= 0.02 \, [(0.8)/(0.2)(0.15)]$$

$$= 0.02 \, (0.8/0.03) = (0.02) \, (26.7)$$

$$= 0.534 \quad (53.4\%)$$

$$\text{Target}_2 = p_{\text{MOQA 2}} \, [E_2/(1 - E_2)]$$
$$= 0.02 \, [0.85/(1 - 0.85)]$$
$$= 0.02 \, (0.85/0.15)$$
$$= 0.02 \, (5.67)$$
$$= 0.113 \quad (11.3\%)$$

Note that the target values in this example are large. This means that the incoming quality at station 1 could be as high as 68%, and the maximum outgoing quality allowed from station 2 of 2% can still be met. However, this requirement is being met with 200% inspection and a large amount of rework and reinspection, clearly a costly method to meet a maximum allowed outgoing quality of 2%.

A better way to meet the allowed quality is to reduce the incoming process defectives. The incoming quality to station 1 must be the same as that to station 2 in order to meet a 2% allowed outgoing level from station 2. The incoming quality to station 1 then would have to be 13.3%. If this is achieved, then station 2 can be reduced to sample inspection or no inspection at all.

Further, when the incoming process defectives to station 1 are reduced to 2%, then it can be considered to change station 1 from 100% inspection to sampling inspection.

Case 3. Two inspection and test stations checking some characteristics that are different and some that are the same.

The outgoing quality for all characteristics at station 2 is computed as follows:

$$p_{\text{out 2}} = p_{\text{out 1A}} + p_{\text{out 2A}} + p_{\text{out 2B}}$$

where $p_{\text{out 1A}}$ is the outgoing quality for the characteristics checked only at station 1

$p_{\text{out 2A}}$ is the outgoing quality for the characteristics checked only at station 2

$p_{\text{out 2B}}$ is the outgoing quality at station 2 for the characteristics checked at both stations

The initial step in determining the targets is to divide the maximum outgoing quality allowed among the three areas (1A, 2A, 2B). The amount assigned to the characteristics checked twice (2B) should be the smallest.

The method for dividing the maximum outgoing quality allowed is the same as described in case 1. Once the outgoing quality allowed for each station is obtained, Eq. (A.2) can be applied to each station for the characteristics that are *different* at each station (set 1A and 2A). The target formula for the characteristics that are checked at both stations can be applied to station 1 and station 2.

Product Flow versus Quality Flow

When these principles are applied to a complex example, the first requirement is to construct a diagram representing the quality flow. Figure A.5 shows an example of the product flow for a final assembly line. Figure A.6 shows the corresponding quality flow.

The quality flow is different from the product flow due to the characteristics being checked at each station. Station 200 checks the same characteristics as stations 155 and 195 combined. Stations 210 and 215 check the same characteristics. Station 155 checks the same characteristics as stations 65, 105, and 150 combined. The duplication of checking characteristics is displayed in Fig. A.6.

Figure A.7 shows the targets required at each station in order to meet the requirement of no more than 1% defective parts going out to the customer. The steps in establishing the targets are outlined below. An effectiveness of 0.8 was used for all stations.

1. Allocate the 1% requirement between stations 200 and 215. 0.8% of the value of the target was assigned to station 200; 0.2% to station 215.

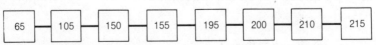

Figure A.5 Product flow.

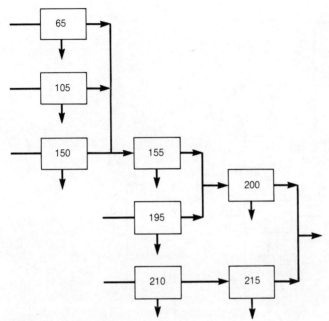

Figure A.6   Quality flow.

2. Calculate the targets for stations 200 and 215 using Eq. (A.2).

3. Compute the incoming quality for stations 200 and 215.

4. Compute the target for station 210 using the incoming quality of 215 and Eq. (A.2).

5. Divide the incoming quality to station 200 between stations 155 and 195.

6. Calculate the targets for stations 155 and 195.

7. Determine the incoming quality for station 155 and divide it among stations 65, 105, and 150.

8. Compute the targets for stations 65, 105, and 150 using Eq. (A.2).

Note that the targets for stations 65 and 105 are large because the same characteristics are checked again at stations 155 and 200, resulting in 300% inspection. If the actual percent defective at stations 65 and 105 is large, then 300% inspection may be required. When the incoming process level at station 65 approaches 5% and the incoming level at station 105 approaches 3%, repeating the inspections at stations 155 and 200 can be reduced or eliminated.

This example shows that the quality target method not only provides

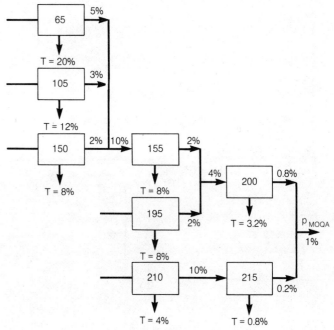

Figure A.7   Quality targets. T stands for target.

the formulas for computing the targets but it also indicates where processes should be improved to reduce or eliminate duplicate inspections.

SUMMARY

Establishing quality targets is a very effective method for finalizing the implementation of SPC. It provides the specific methods needed to meet customer requirements.

Conclusion

The objective of this text was to provide an understanding of statistical process control to executives and their staff so they may use it to lead their organizations to success. Case studies were reviewed that demonstrated how productivity improvement was achieved. The methods were described, and all that really remains for an organization is the spark of executive desire to put them into effect.

The implementation requirements of a successful PQI process were discussed throughout the chapters:

1. Obtain upper management's understanding, commitment, participation, and support.

2. Educate the appropriate people in statistical techniques, problem-solving techniques, quality planning, and PQI leadership.

3. Create an implementation plan including an organizational structure for teams, steering committees, and an executive board.

4. Implement the PQI process using the systematic approach, which promotes a focused, hands-on, proactive effort.

This text does not replace the value and benefits of live instruction and reinforcement by facilitation. Consistent education, demonstration, coaching, and auditing are essential to successful implementation and sustainment of the PQI process.

When these 12 steps are systematically implemented with discipline, outstanding results can be achieved. Once the initial targets are met, new targets are formulated and a continuous improvement process is established. The main objectives of the PQI process are the reduction of variability, intolerance to defects and errors, and continuous improvement. When these attitudes are installed in an organization and the methods provided, the process transforms the organization's culture for the better.

Glossary

Advanced Statistical Methods. More sophisticated and less widely applicable techniques of statistical process analysis and control than are included in basic statistical methods; examples are advanced control chart techniques, regression analysis, design of experiments, and advanced problem-solving techniques.

Attribute Data. Qualitative data that can be counted for recording and analysis. Attribute data are usually gathered in the form of nonconforming units or of nonconformities; they are analyzed by p, np, c, and u control charts.

Average. The sum of values divided by the number (sample size) of values, and designated by a bar over the symbol (e.g., $\overline{X}$). (See also Mean.)

Awareness. Personal understanding of the interrelationship of quality and productivity.

Basic Statistical Methods. Applies the theory of variation through basic problem-solving techniques and statistical process control; includes control chart construction and interpretation (for both variable and attribute data) and capability analysis.

Capability. (Can be determined only after the process is in statistical control.) When the process average plus and minus the 3-σ spread of the distribution of individuals is contained within the specification tolerance (variable data), or when at least 99.73% of individuals are within specification (attribute data), a process is capable.

Cause-and-Effect Diagram. A simple tool for individual or group problem solving that uses a graphic description of the various process elements to analyze potential sources of process variation. Also called a fishbone diagram (after its appearance) or Ishikawa diagram (after its developer).

Center Line. The line on a control chart that represents the average or median value of the items being plotted.

Characteristic. A distinguishing feature of a process or its output on which variable or attribute data can be collected.

Common Cause. A source of variation that affects all values of the process output being studied; in control chart analysis it appears as part of the random process variation.

Consecutive Units. Units of output produced in succession; a basis for selecting subgroup samples.

Control. See Statistical Control.

Control Chart. A graphic representation of a characteristic of a process, showing plotted values of some statistic gathered from that characteristic, a center line, and one or two control limits. It minimizes the net economic loss from type I and type II errors. It has two basic uses: as a judgment to determine if a process has been operating in statistical control, and as an operation to aid in maintaining statistical control.

Control Limit. A line (or lines) on a control chart used as a basis for judging the significance of the variation from subgroup to subgroup. Variation beyond a control limit is evidence that special causes are affecting the process. Control limits are calculated from process data and are not to be confused with engineering specifications.

Detection. A past-oriented strategy that attempts to identify unacceptable output after it has been produced and to separate it from the good output. (See also Prevention.)

Distribution. A way of describing the output of a common-cause system of variation, in which individual values are not predictable but in which the outcomes as a group form a pattern that can be described in terms of its location, spread, and shape. Location is commonly expressed by the mean (average) or by the median; spread by the standard deviation or the range of a sample; and shape by the normal, binominal, or Poisson distributions.

Individual. A single unit or a single measurement of a characteristic.

Location. A general concept for the typical values or central tendency of a distribution.

Mean. The average of values in a group of measurements.

Median. The middle value in a group of measurements, when arranged from lowest to highest; if the number of values is even, then by convention the average of the middle two values is used as the median.

Performance Improvement Process. The operational philosophy within a company to produce products of increasing quality for its customers in an increasingly efficient way that protects the return on investment to its stockholders.

Nonconforming Units. Units that do not conform to a specification or other inspection standard; sometimes called discrepant or defective units.

Nonconformities. Specific occurrences of a condition that does not conform to specifications or other inspection standards; sometimes called discrepancies or defects.

Normal Distribution. A continuous, symmetrical, bell-shaped frequency distribution for variable data that underlies the control charts for variables. When measurements have a normal distribution, about 68.26% of all individuals lie within plus or minus one standard deviation unit of the mean, 95.44%

lie within plus and minus two standard deviation units of the mean, and about 99.73% lie within plus and minus three standard deviation units of the mean.

Normal Probability Paper. Paper whose lines are spaced according to the normal distribution along the ordinate and equally spaced along the abscissa.

Operational Definition. A means of clearly communicating quality expectations and performance; it consists of (1) a criterion to be applied to an object or to a group, (2) a test of the object or of the group, and (3) a decision as to whether the object or the group met the criterion.

Pareto Chart. A simple tool for problem solving that involves ranking all potential problem areas or sources of variation according to their contribution to cost or to total variation.

Prevention. A future-oriented strategy that improves productivity and quality by directing analysis and action toward correcting the process itself. (See also Detection.)

Problem Solving. The process of moving from symptoms to causes (special or common) to actions that improve performance.

Process. The combination of people, equipment, materials, methods, and environment that produces output—a given product or service.

Process Average. The location of the distribution of measured values of a particular process characteristic.

Process Control. See Statistical Process Control.

Process Spread. The extent to which the distributions of individual values of the process characteristic vary.

Randomness. A condition in which individual values are not predictable, although they may come from a definable distribution.

Range. The difference between the highest and lowest values in a subgroup.

Run. A consecutive number of points consistently increasing or decreasing, or above or below the center line.

Run Chart. A simple graphic representation of a characteristic or a process showing plotted values of some statistic gathered from the process (often individual values) and a center line (often the median of the values) that can be analyzed for runs. (See also Control Chart.)

Sample. In process control applications, a synonym for subgroup.

Shape. A general concept for the overall pattern formed by a distribution of values.

Sigma (σ). The Greek letter used to designate a standard deviation.

Special Cause. A source of variation that is intermittent, unpredictable, unstable; sometimes called an assignable cause.

Spread. A general concept for the extent by which values in a distribution differ from one another. Also called dispersion.

Stability.   The absence of special causes of variation; the property of being in statistical control.

Stable Process.   A process in statistical control.

Standard Deviation.   A measure of the spread of the process output or the spread of a sampling statistic from the process.

Statistic.   A value calculated from or based upon sample data and used to make inferences about the process that produced the output from which the sample came.

Statistical Control.   The condition describing a process from which all special causes of variation have been eliminated and only common causes remain; evidenced on a control chart by the absence of points beyond the control limits and by the absence of nonrandom patterns or trends within the control limits.

Statistical Process Control.   The use of statistical techniques such as control charts to analyze a process or its outputs so as to take appropriate action to achieve and maintain a state of statistical control and to improve the process capability.

Subgroup.   One or more events or measurements used to analyze the performance of a process. Rational subgroups are usually chosen so that the variation represented within each subgroup is as small as feasible for the process (representing the variation from common causes) and so that any changes in the process performance (i.e., special causes) will appear as differences between subgroups. Rational subgroups are typically made up of consecutive pieces, although random samples are sometimes used.

Type I Error.   Taking action appropriate for a special cause when in fact the process has not changed; overcontrol.

Type II Error.   Not taking appropriate action when in fact the process is affected by special causes; undercontrol.

Variable Data.   Quantitative data, where measurements are used for analysis.

Variation.   The inevitable differences among individual outputs of a process; the sources of variation can be grouped into two major classes: common causes and special causes.

List of Symbols

A_2	A multiplier used to calculate the control limits for averages.
d_2	A divisor of R used to estimate the process standard deviation.
D_3, D_4	Multiples of R used to calculate the lower and upper control limits, respectively, for ranges.
k	The number of subgroups being used to calculate control limits.
LCL	The lower control limit; LCL_X, LCL_R, and LCL_p are, respectively, the lower control limits for averages, ranges, and proportion nonconforming.
n	The number of individuals in a subgroup; the subgroup sample size.
$\bar{n}$	The average subgroup sample size.
np	The number of nonconforming items in a sample of size n.
$\bar{n}$p	The average number of nonconforming items in samples of constant size n.
p	The proportion of units nonconforming in a sample.
$\bar{p}$	The average proportion of units nonconforming in a series of samples (weighted by sample size).
R	The subgroup range (highest value minus lowest value).
$\bar{R}$	The average range of a series of subgroups of constant size.
u	The number of nonconformities per unit in a sample that may contain more than one unit.
$\bar{u}$	The average number of nonconformities per unit in samples not necessarily of the same size.
UCL	The upper control limit.
X	An individual value upon which other subgroup statistics are based.
$\bar{X}$	The average of values in a subgroup.
$\bar{\bar{X}}$	The average of subgroup averages (weighted if necessary by sample size); the measured process average.
σ	The standard deviation of the distribution of individual values of a process characteristic.
$\hat{\sigma}$	An estimate of the standard deviation of a process characteristic.

Bibliography

Crosby, Philip B.: *Quality Without Tears: The Art of Hassle-Free Management*, McGraw-Hill, New York, 1984.

Deming, W. Edwards: *Quality, Productivity, and Competitive Position*, Center for Advanced Engineering Study, Cambridge, Massachusetts, 1982.

Grant, Eugene L. and Richard Leavenworth: *Statistical Quality Control*, 5th ed., McGraw-Hill, New York, 1979.

Hale, Guy A.: *Process Management Skills*, Alamo Learning Systems, Inc., Walnut Creek, California, 1982.

Juran, Joseph M.: *Upper Management and Quality*, 3rd ed., Juran Institute, Danbury, Connecticut, 1982.

Juran, Joseph M. and Frank M. Gryna, Jr.: *Quality Planning and Analysis: From Product Development Through Use*, 2nd ed., McGraw-Hill, New York, 1980.

Plunkett, Lorne C. and Guy A. Hale: *The Proactive Manager: The Complete Book of Problem-Solving and Decision-Making*, John Wiley, New York, 1982.

Index

ABOUT THE AUTHOR

Jack Hradesky has 25 years of experience in the areas of productivity and quality improvement and cost savings programs at such firms as Eastman Kodak, Xerox, General Motors, American Hospital Supply, and Johnson & Johnson. He had held a variety of positions ranging from director of manufacturing and plant quality manager to material operations manager and plant operator before founding his own consulting firm, National Summit Group, in 1981. Now a consultant to Hughes Aircraft, McDonnell-Douglas Computer System Company, Printronix, and others, Mr. Hradesky is a registered professional engineer and a member of the American Society for Quality Control and the American Production and Inventory Control Society.